Our Doggie Delinquents

Did We Reform Them? Or Did They Reform Us?

Best wishes!
Kathy Boettcher

Kathy Boettcher

CELEEN PUBLISHING
Dog Tales Division
San Diego, California

CELEEN PUBLISHING
Dog Tales Division
P. O. Box 928049
San Diego, CA 92192-8049 USA

This book is autobiographical. Names have been changed to protect the innocent.

Library of Congress Control Number: 2003097069

ISBN 0-9637557-1-4

Cover design by Cheryl Staples
Book design and production by Cheryl and Brian Staples
Back cover photo by Gregory Gilgen

Library of Congress Cataloging-in-Publication Data

Boettcher, Kathleen S.
Our Doggie Delinquents / by Kathy Boettcher
p. cm.
Summary: Autobiographical. Discusses the author's decision to own and raise a variety of dogs, and its impact on the lives of family and friends.
ISBN 0-9637557-1-4 (papercover : alk. paper)

2003097069

Printed in the United States of America

Acknowledgements

A special thanks to the following people who took the time to read my manuscript and made comments that helped refine the final edition:

Boots and Jim Shepherd
Mary and John Seul
Melissa and Rus Engel
Robin Little
Debra Bax
Nancy Russell
Sue Orgas
Jeri El Dissi
Wanda Delopst
Geri Boettcher
Ruby Marshall
Bruce Boettcher
Sheri Boettcher
Jason Boettcher
Karen Pollock
Ann Trimmer, DVM
Dave and Julie Christensen
Suzanne Frank
Joan and Collette Morgan
Dennis Napier
Jane Petitmermet
Paula Thompson
Alexis Borich
Donna Neuhauser
Joann Ramsthaler

I also wish to thank the members of the following organizations:

The Siberian Husky Club of Greater Milwaukee
The Siberian Husky Club of Greater Chicago
The Waukesha Kennel Club
The Siberian Husky Club of America

I met many people in the above organizations who taught me and encouraged me. They impacted my life in a myriad of ways. Though we came from many different backgrounds, we had one thing in common: our love of dogs.

Dedicated to

Dorothy Page

Dorothy encouraged me to write down my "doggie" experiences over twenty years ago. She saw a writer and a storyteller when I did not. I appreciate her confidence that I could change my spoken words into print on a page. Her dedication to the sport of dogs, appreciation and love of the Siberian Husky, fantastic sense of humor, willingness to share her expertise with a novice, and her knowledge set her apart. How do you thank someone who has encouraged you to learn, use your eyes, listen to your intuition, and find a talent you didn't know you had? I think you simply say...thank you, Dorothy.

Love,
Kathy

In Loving Memory of

James Robert "Bob" Page

Breeder, owner, handler of CH CHOTOVOTKA's Ms. Kitty Russell (Siberian Husky). AKC Licensed Dog Show Judge. A good man and great friend.

Karen Webb

Owner and handler of CH NORSKA's Mishka (Siberian Husky). You taught me many things about dogs and life. We traveled the path of "dogdom" together. Thank you for your friendship.

Preface

It all began with a great idea. Our family would add a loyal canine companion. A tiny bundle of fur who would love us as much as we loved him. We would romp together, hang out together, and share life's adventures. Grateful for the opportunity to join such a special family, he would spend evenings curled up at our feet while we all sat in front of a crackling fire enjoying our bond of love. Boy, when I create a fantasy, I create an exceptional one.

And ponder this. Why would loving pet owners become "show dog" people? Do they "turn" under a full moon like some demented werewolf? Does their focus shift, in the blink of an eye, from normal routines to obsessions with crates, grooming supplies, leashes, training, and such? Or, is it a slow slide into chaos?

Perhaps my story will give you insight into a world of unusual challenges and loving canine companionship. Here is a peek at my own journey into what those watching must have thought was..."insanity." Maybe it was. But, it was a wonderful, exciting trip.

The dogs with whom my small family shared life taught us many things and changed me forever. They put me on a path I never envisioned possible. My heart filled with love for past friends, human and animal, as I wrote about these memories. May our experiences fill your heart with joy, laughter, and love as you see city folks transformed into...something quite different.

I wish to share that time with you.

Kathy Boettcher

What others are saying about this book

"Kathy Boettcher has put the "WOW" in Bow Wow with her new book about life with dogs. Or is it rather dogs with life! Either way, the book is a rompin' read and a heart-warming hiatus into all things that verify 'a dog is a (wo)man's best friend'. The truth is, only with friends would you do some of those antics! I recommend it highly." "Frankly Fond of Dogs" aka Suzanne Frank, Waukesha, Wisconsin.

"This story is full of joy and mischief. I laughed out loud so many times. Kathy Boettcher has such a unique look at life you can't help but be touched. Even if you're not an animal lover, you just might be converted after reading this book." Karen Pollock, animal lover, Clairemont, California.

"A true story told from the heart as only Kathy can tell it. Funny, heartfelt, with a lesson in what dogs and people are all about." Mary and John Seul, Keenonne Kennels, Chicago, Illinois.

"This touching collection of stories perfectly captures the joy and happiness a pet brings to their owner's life. They leave the reader with a smile on their face." Ann Trimmer, DVM, San Diego, California.

"Reading this book was so much fun. It was so vivid, as if you were watching a movie—the adventures of one family and their dogs. We laughed at the hijinks the animals put the family through and the unique ways they coped with all of them. We thoroughly enjoyed the way it was told." Melissa and Rus Engel, people who enjoy real-life humor, Waukesha, Wisconsin.

"This book is truly delightful. I lived each chapter with the Boettcher family. I will reread this book many times. Kathy, you have brought all the trials and tribulations of owning and loving our dogs to print." Debra Bax, owner and trainer of agility titled dogs. Recently lost Chance's Fate, CDX, MX, MXJ–a dog who changed her life. Lakeside, California.

"I loved this book. It is full of laughter and information galore. Being with this family and their dogs is fantastic! So real and truthful. Our lives with dogs is so incredible. Thanks Kathy. Four paws up." Robin Little, all-breed dog groomer, Robin's Doghouse, San Diego, California.

"Our Doggie Delinquents is a delightful, heart-warming read. Even non-dog lovers will enjoy the antics of the dogs—and the humans!" Jane Petitmermet, retired librarian, University City, California.

"I laughed and laughed about the all-too-familiar doggie shenanigans! These stories are an absolute gold mine to fellow dog lovers." Wanda Delopst, dog lover, La Mesa, California.

"This book should be on every coffee table. It's a thoroughly enjoyable and funny read." Boots Shepherd, Cadoga Siberians, Fond du Lac, Wisconsin. Past president of the Siberian Husky Club of Greater Milwaukee; past conformation, obedience, and Junior Showmanship trainer; past chairman/co-chair of approximately 25 AKC dog shows; past 4-H Dog Project Leader; past Siberian Husky breeder and exhibitor.

"I found this book to be especially funny since I grew up in the 'dog show world'. And, because I deal with so many newcomers in my business, I can find so much humor in her writing. This book is a must read for any 'doggy person'. It will bring a smile to your face and put a laugh in your heart for days after you read it." Jeri El Dissi, Waukesha, Wisconsin. Professional dog handler and owner of LDC Professional Pet Products.

Foreword

"I laughed, giggled, or smiled as I read each doggy dilemma. For those of us who own Northern breeds, you will laugh and nod your head "yes" as you recall similar situations in the past. Kathy slips in tidbits of wisdom and good advice on buying and raising dogs. For dog lovers of all ages this will be a fun book to read."

Nancy C. Russell

Storm Kloud Kennel, Alaskan Malamutes

Breeder of 197 AKC Champions including 144 Best in Show on 6 Continents
Professional Dog Handler (25 years)
AKC judge (3 years)
Humane Officer town of Lisbon and Village of Sussex (23 years)
Waukesha Kennel Club member (35 years) AKC Delegate
Alaskan Malamute Club of America-Past President and member (40 years)
Wisconsin Alaskan Malamute Club-founding member
Dog Handlers Guild member (12 years)
Humane Animal Welfare Society of Waukesha County (Board of Directors 3 years)

Chapter One

It began thirty years ago in Waukesha, Wisconsin. I like to think I was a fairly intelligent, relatively sane woman. I suppose some would disagree, but work with me here. Indulge me. I was thirty years old, married to a CPA named Bruce, and had two children, Sheri and Jason. Sheri was seven and Jason two. I was a stay-at-home mom and enjoyed being one. We had a tiny house with a small yard on a quiet street. Life was good, stress-free, and normal. We were average people living average lives. I was about to change all that.

I decided our family needed an addition—a cute, cuddly puppy. Bruce and the kids enthusiastically agreed. We went to the Humane Society and checked out the dog population. A kind Humane Society volunteer asked me what breed of dog I was looking for.

I frowned and said, "You mean they come in different flavors? I thought they just came in different sizes."

She rolled her eyes and explained that there were over one hundred different breeds. She suggested I go to the library and get *The American Kennel Club's Complete Dog Book*. This book had photos and descriptions of every breed. I took her advice and discovered that each breed was created for a specific purpose. The book advised that, when deciding on a breed, you should take into consideration what the dog was bred to do and its needs. Some require lots of attention, some hardly any. Some need lots of room to run and romp, some do fine in a house or apartment. Some need lots of attention, some are independent. And, if these facts are taken into consideration before you select a dog, many problems can be averted. It's easy to fall in love with a breed because they're pretty or cute or tough looking, but that's not the proper criteria for making a choice.

I thought, I can be a proper selector of dogs and make an intelligent choice based on the dog's needs and ours. I've done my homework. I understand this process. If I do a good job, and I will, having a dog won't impact our lives in any way. That last statement is called being "naïve." Combined with overconfidence, it can come back to bite you on the behind. I'm telling you this from personal experience.

I analyzed our small tribe's personalities, my children's ages, and our living arrangements, then tried to match this information with a breed of dog. I decided we needed a dog that was small, tough, loved children, didn't rattle easily, and would act as a barking burglar alarm. It seemed that a West Highland White Terrier (called a Westie for short) was the perfect choice.

We went back to the Humane Society. Much to my disappointment, they did not have Westies or small dogs of any kind.

I searched the classified ads and found nothing.

I asked friends. They had never heard of a Westie and asked what was wrong with a mutt? I said, "Nothing was wrong with a mutt, but I can't seem to find the right kind."

So, off we went to the pet store. (I didn't know about dog shows or how to contact breeders.)

There, sitting in a cage, was the cutest West Highland White Terrier on the planet. His black eyes sparkled with intelligence. His tail and entire behind wagged with enthusiasm. His whole body oozed playfulness. We bought him on the spot.

We happily purchased the necessary puppy supplies, took our puppy home, and named him Boettcher's Jack Frost—Frosty for short. We proudly sent our West Highland White Terrier's official registration paper to the American Kennel Club (AKC) for proper recording.

Frosty had hutzpah and no fear. He explored for brief periods of time, didn't get into any mischief, and loved each one of us. He seemed docile after each short play period and learned our routine quickly. I thought, This puppy stuff is easy.

The imp of a puppy had stolen our hearts.

After two days, Frosty began coughing, seemed to lose his sparkle, and laid around listlessly. I feared he might be sick and made my first veterinarian appointment. The diagnosis was kennel cough.

Dr. Vet also explained that Frosty was overshot and that was a serious fault. I hated to admit I didn't know what "overshot" or "serious fault" were, but 'fessed up. I suppose it was in the American Kennel Club book, but I must have zipped over that part. Zipping over facts has always been a "fault" of mine.

Dr. Vet explained Frosty's front teeth did not close in a proper scissors bite. I thought, Okay. No big deal. As long as he can chew and swallow, we won't worry. I learned later that there are good reasons a bad bite is a fault in many breeds, but let's apply this just to Frosty. Think of it this way. If your Terrier had a scrapping, angry rat in his mouth and the nasty thing slithered out and bit your nose because the dog's teeth weren't tight, how big of a deal would it be? Now, apply that logic to other breeds and you get the drift. There are also other reasons, but I won't go into them here.

Dr. Vet had checked the puppy's front end, now he was checking the back end. He scowled, sighed, and announced that Frosty had one descended testicle that should be removed. The other testicle was retained in the body. You modern, enlightened folks cannot imagine how naïve I was in the 1970s. I had never heard the word "testicle" whispered in private, much less discussed it, or them, with a stranger. And, I didn't know dogs were supposed to have two. As Dr. Vet explained, a red blush crept up my neck and face. I've always blushed at the drop of a hat or "the drop of a testicle," which in this case hadn't. Dropped, that is.

While discussing testicles and neutering with this man I had just met, I tried to look worldly and appear unruffled. I probably didn't pull it off because I still can't pull it off. Dr. Vet explained the advantages of neutering and said the retained testicle should also be removed because it could become cancerous. I agreed to have Frosty neutered when he was old enough.

We moved on to Frosty's treatment for kennel cough. It consisted of pills and instruction on how to hold him over a vaporizer to help with the coughing.

I tucked Frosty under one arm, collected his pills, paid the bill and, when the receptionist asked if I was all right because my face was flushed, I muttered something about windburn from the day before and hurried out. I apologized to Frosty several times for agreeing to remove his manhood. Bruce paled when I told him what Dr. Vet wanted to do. Frosty didn't seem to care.

I immediately pulled out the family vaporizer and every few hours, day and night, dangled Frosty over the steam. Sheri had bronchial hay fever, and I had used the vaporizer many times to relieve her congestion. However, she laid in bed, and I did not have to dangle her. I never really appreciated Sheri's skill in being treated until Frosty came along. How can a dog be harder to take care of than a child? That question has plagued me to this day.

After a week of sleepless nights, I decided this puppy stuff was too much like having a new baby. Then, in a flash of amazing insight, I realized that's exactly what I had—a new baby.

Frosty began to improve. On the surface, that seems like wonderful news. But, did you know a sick dog is also a quiet, docile dog? That is, unless you're dangling him over a vaporizer, and he's wiggling and squirming to get down. I followed Dr. Vet's instructions to the letter. I was determined to be a healer of small dogs, and my dedication paid off.

As Frosty's strength returned, so did his desire to take on the world. Everything in sight was fair game for his inquisitive little black nose and four paws. It seems that his congenial, cooperative attitude was a result of being sick and not an indicator of his true personality. And, thanks to my skill as a fledgling vet assistant, Frosty was healed! He now had unbelievable energy! His original short romps turned into long, untiring ones. My little gentleman turned into a demon on paws.

Frosty's recovery was amazing. He seemed determined to be busy every moment and make up for lost time. We thought, How cute! Look, he's dragging a shoe around that's bigger than he is. Hey! Give me that! Hey! Come back here with that! Don't chew on it! Oh, no! My best shoes have been reconfigured!

Look, he climbs and jumps on everything! Even tall chairs and beds. What an amazing guy. No! Don't dig in the furniture! Don't dig in the bed! You'll tear...oh well. The bedspread was old. He barks at the mailman. That's great! He'll keep intruders away. Okay, Frosty! That's enough. The mailman's a good guy. Frosty, stop that barking. Be good. Frosty! Shut up!

He's inquisitive and sniffing in every corner. That shows he's smart! Hey! Stop that! Don't do that in the corner! Oh, yuck! We do that outside!

He's admiring the plant in my big pot on the floor. What a cute guy. Hey! No! Don't dig in that! Oh, my goodness, don't eat the plant! It might be poisonous for puppies, and I'll be a killer! Get away from that pot! Oh, no! Look at the carpet and your face and feet, young man! What a mess! Don't dig in the pot! Don't eat the greenery. I'm not that good at growing it! Hmm. I suppose I could put the pot on a shelf instead of the floor. No! We don't dig holes in the yard, either! My goodness! Look how deep that hole is and where did the dirt go! Stop it! You'll bury yourself!

I took our precious bundle of energy to my mother's to show him off. Now, Mom was not a dog lover and had never allowed us to have one. She was not thrilled when I brought "that animal" into her kitchen. She closed the sliding door to the rest of the house and sternly announced we were restricted to the kitchen. I wasn't particularly upset by this, because she also restricted Jason and his chocolate cookie hands to the kitchen.

However, I could not believe the crabby way she reacted when Frosty enthusiastically slopped water from his drinking bowl onto her floor, then, a few minutes later, marked this new territory. Now, granted, she did slip in his piddle puddle. And she had just scrubbed the kitchen floor. But, I cleaned up both the clean water and the recycled water. She did not seem amused when I quipped that it was a good thing Frosty had lapped up so much water because the urine was diluted and didn't smell as bad as it usually did. Oh, well. Some people do not have a sense of humor.

Of course, my Mom had been dealing with my rather warped sense of humor and weird perspective on life for a very long time.

Frosty was a tiny bundle of energy. His favorite game was to steal my fuzzy pink slipper and kill it. He'd attack that slipper with the gusto of a game-killing cheetah. Frosty would stalk the slipper, pounce, and shake the life out of it. This was no small feat as my "feet" are substantial. When I lamented about their size, Mom always told me that tall buildings need substantial foundations. If a girl of my height of 5´7˝ had tiny feet, she'd flop over. I had long ago decided to take her counsel but, I confess, watching the tiny Frosty trying to dispatch my size ten slippers did open the "size" issue once again.

While I taught Frosty that shoes were out of bounds, I admit I encouraged him to play the slipper game. It was hilarious to watch. Frosty would shake that slipper so hard it would flop from side to side. His growls of attack were not to be taken lightly, especially if you were a flopping slipper. I decided that Westies are bred to hunt varmints and my slippers were, hopefully, as close as he'd ever get to one. He needed the "kill the slipper" game to quell his natural instincts to stalk and hunt furry things and to keep his psyche healthy.

Now, granted, my slippers did get a trifle stiff from dog spit and lost their fuzzy luster. And, true, they started to look a bit bedraggled from being killed over and over again.

But, the biggest problem came when Frosty decided to attack while the slippers were on my feet. I'd walk. He'd stalk me, then attack and latch onto one with fervor. Now, he had a moving target! What fun! I'd hobble around the house, dragging Frosty along with me while he growled, hung on for dear life, and tried desperately to shake the defiant slipper. I loved doing it.

Oh, there were days when it got a little wearisome dragging a growling dog along the floor, especially when he got full grown. But, he eventually grew tired of the game. I think he was three or four years old by that time and had gone on to larger prey. That prey being our growing pack of Siberian Huskies. They considered the barking, yapping Westie nipping at their heels a nuisance to be tolerated. He considered them the best prey in the world!

The other game Frosty enjoyed was "attack the vacuum cleaner." Every time I vacuumed, Frosty leapt at the cleaner, barking and growling. Again, I tolerated his antics. First, because I admired his courage even though I questioned his intelligence. And, second, because I still thought he needed to express his instincts. I know there are dog trainers out there who would disagree, but I long ago decided that as long as I, personally, could tolerate the behaviors I encouraged and they weren't bothersome or a nuisance to anyone else, then I would enjoy my dogs in the way I saw fit. The "not bothersome or a nuisance to anyone else" is extremely important. Frosty killed only my slippers and attacked only my vacuum cleaner, not anyone else's.

We were thrilled with our new family member, and, to show our gratitude for his antics and entertainment, we bought a spiffy dog bed. It had a red metal frame and big soft pillow. Of course, it was way too big, but we didn't care. A true friend should have a luxurious bed to stretch out in.

He loved the kids, and they loved him. Everything seemed perfect with this bundle of white energy. Then, it happened. Our cuddly puppy turned into a...dog!

Frosty started lifting his leg to show his developing masculinity. Wow! He has amazing range for such a small guy. And, look at his cute little swagger. Wait a minute, Frosty! We don't do that on the corner of the bedspread. We know you're just a baby, but we don't do that on the corner of the sofa, either. Or, the chair. We do that outside against a post or the house or a bush or a tree. I explained to him that these were viable alternatives.

And, you never, never do that other suggestive thing to Jason's foot or Sheri's leg! Shame on you!

He wagged his tail and I thought, Good going! You just talk to the little guy the way you do the children and explain the rules. That seems like a reasonable approach.

But, guess what? There was a flaw in that logic. Let's analyze. Did my lecturing the children always have a positive result? For that matter, did explaining my reasons affect Bruce's outlook? Actually, occasionally, they acted just like Frosty. Big grin, nod of understanding, and unspoken agreement, then do exactly the opposite. Why did I expect the end result to be any different with the dog than it was with my family? Add in the language barrier and did my common sense step out to lunch? They say we learn from experience. I'm not so sure.

I was as patient with Frosty as I was with Bruce, Sheri, and Jason. I said, with a smile, "Frosty, no. Do not lift on the bedspread. It makes a nasty smell, so you do that outdoors." I moved on to, "Frosty, no! Outside!" Then to, "Frosty, NO!!!!" Then to, "Frosty, blast you, NO!!!!! Get your white, furry behind...OUTSIDE!!!!!!"

At that point, he stopped lifting. Imagine that! I trained him! I showed him...outside...and he understood people language! I did have to watch his every move, but I was willing to take what I could get. He'd glance over his shoulder at me and, if I was watching, do that cute little Westie grin, wag his tail, and move to the door. Then...outside...we went, and he did his business. I was so proud of myself. I had actually housebroken a dog! As a much older, wiser individual, I will consider the point that, perhaps, just perhaps, the dog had trained me.

Several weeks later, I decided to launder the bedspread. I picked it up and scowled. Hmmm. The bottom corner end seems stiff. Why would the bedspread be stiff? That makes no sense. I held it up to scrutinize the cloth and winced from the smell. My highly intellectual ability went into full throttle. Stiff? Bad smell? FROSTY!!!!

It seems my little friend wasn't trained. He just got sneakier! Or, maybe he was trained. Trained to assess "marking" conditions and, craftily, go behind my back. But, I decided I was smarter than that little critter and came up with a plan. I kept the bedroom door shut and dwindled his territory to just three very small rooms—our tiny living room, kitchen, and the kids' bedroom. That put our bedspread out of his territory. I admit that I finally had to close the kid's bedroom door, too, because even though our bedspread was his first choice, apparently theirs was a viable substitute. But, now I had that varmint under control! Well, sort of. I suppose, in an honest discussion regarding the true definition of "under control," my success might be questioned. Whenever he got the chance, Frosty marked the corner of bedspreads until his dying day. Funny thing, though. No one ever caught him doing it. There was, however, a downside to shutting doors. I started feeling claustrophobic.

Frosty did respect my wishes when it came to being friendly with feet and legs. That might have been a direct result of neutering, but I prefer to think it was about me being boss and a superb trainer.

Then, we began discovering little brown "presents" when we returned from errands. Oh, blast, what now? I astutely ascertained that I couldn't watch his every move when I wasn't there.

I know! I'll put a board between the kitchen and living room. That will confine Frosty to the kitchen when we're gone. We'll put newspapers down for him to put his presents on. End of problem!

That worked. For about ten days. We came home from Granny's one night and stepped into the kitchen. Oh, my God! Frosty's gone! Frosty! Frosty! Oh, no! Someone broke in and dognapped Frosty!

I'm not sure if I felt relief, or the desire to kill, when he peeked over the board and gave us that, "Hi, guys, where you been?" Westie grin. His tail was wagging triumphantly as he stood on his back feet, hooked his front feet over the board, and peered at us from the living room.

I scowled at him, but thought, Calm down. He wasn't dognapped and the papers aren't soiled. These are good things. At least, he's figured out to wait to answer nature's call. I ask you, how could I be so blasted naïve? When God handed out smarts, where was I? Probably in a corner petting some kitten instead of listening and paying attention!

I stepped over the board. A brown present and puddle waited. Oh, now I get it. He didn't want to mess his kitchen living quarters, so he...FROSTY!!!

I blew a strand of fallen hair off my forehead and decided, I'm not defeated yet.

I got a higher board. This one was almost up to my knees and Frosty was not that tall. Ah-hah! I've got you this time, you delinquent!

It worked. For a few weeks. Then, we found him in the living room again with another brown "present."

This dog is not going to outsmart me! Get a higher board. Use your brain! Humans have more intelligence than dogs! That's what all the books say!

The higher board worked. For a while. One day, I was sitting in the living room watching *Tarzan* on TV (my favorite program) when I heard this funny noise. I had put Frosty in the kitchen behind his board, so I didn't have to watch his every move. I wanted to watch Tarzan's every muscled move.

Frosty was perched on top of the board. I actually had the presence of mind to take a picture. It's in our family album under the "Frosty wins and outsmarts Mom" section. Incidentally, that section is thicker than I care to admit.

Frosty wobbled on top of the board, frantically clawing to get over the top for a few moments, then leapt into the living room, raced across the floor and jumped up onto the furniture. Then, it occurred to me that the furniture was higher than the board. Why did I think that a barrier lower than the furniture he leapt onto with ease was going to contain him? More flawed logic. I gave up and held him on my lap while I watched Tarzan swing from tree to tree.

As I really didn't like what the board did for my decor, I came up with another solution. That, by the way, is the greatest gift my dogs have given me. The motivation to come up with "another solution." Here was mine. Originally, there was a door between the living room and the kitchen, but closing it made the house seem like a monk's cell, so we had taken it off in an effort to make the house seem larger.

Problem? I needed something very high that would open and close and not make the house dark and dreary. I pondered for a few hours, then came up with a terrific idea! I would saw the door in half, make it about chest high, use two of the hinges on the original door, put a little shelf on top, and have a homemade Dutch door without the upper "Dutch." I mentally high-fived myself. That's a brilliant sollution!

Bruce wasn't so sure my idea was "brilliant," but I talked him into it and convinced my CPA husband, who disliked fix-it projects of any kind with a passion, that we could do it. Neither one of us had done anything like it before, but how hard could it be? I'll give you a hint as to the answer. Harder than we thought.

Bruce and I actually work pretty well together on projects. I admit I'm inclined to get a little snotty when things don't go exactly the way I think they should and take hours longer than I planned. And, Bruce is a little impatient with my tendency to omit reading directions and just "do it." The trouble with "just doing it" is we often have extra parts or get to "do it" over again. But, what's the big deal? Bruce is good at figuring out where those extra parts should have gone. And, my opinion is, if you have an extra part and the gizmo you're working on does what it's supposed to do, the extra part probably wasn't necessary in the first place. Bruce grits his teeth in the cutest way when I say that.

I have apologized a zillion times for my smart aleck remarks, lecturing tone, and disgusted sighs during projects. I'm really an easy going kind of gal, not short tempered in any way. I was shocked when, a few months ago, my adult daughter fled the house when she found out Bruce and I were taking on a project. I asked her what prompted that behavior? She muttered something about her nerves.

Back to the door. After a few hours of "gentle" conversation and hard work, it was finished. We sawed, we sandpapered, we pounded, we got the door back onto its hinges. And—the door actually opened and closed! We were so proud of our accomplishment. And, Bruce and I had worked together without killing each other! Wow! See what little Frosty had accomplished? His spirit of adventure forced us to be creative and work together. Little did we know we were setting a precedent.

Bruce and I were happy with our project. We had a renovated short door made out of a long door that actually opened and shut like it should. We added a shelf to the top and were slightly astounded that my idea worked. The next time we ran errands, we left Frosty behind our amazing new door, and I was feeling smug and definitely in control. When we returned, we stepped into the kitchen, and it looked like a blizzard had hit!

Apparently, Frosty decided to show his displeasure at our success. He shredded his spiffy bed. There was shredded white pillow stuffing everywhere. And, to top it off, Frosty was gone. I could not believe my eyes! Surely, he didn't scale that door!

I called him. He meandered out from under a cupboard. The previous owners had taken the dishwasher with them and left a hole. I had put a lovely little curtain over the opening and used it for storage. Frosty decided it was his new lair.

Okay, little varmint! No more bed. Sleep on the blasted floor like a dog! Who cares!

I did relent slightly and put a nice soft rug in the hole behind the curtain. Anyone see what had happened here? I'll give you a clue. My storage area had become an inside doghouse. Who actually won that round? Had I been outwitted by a pile of fur?

The next day, I was in front of our house mowing the lawn. Our front yard sloped sharply upward and the house sat on a tiny hill. I looked at the kitchen window that faced the front yard and smiled. Frosty was looking out at me. How cute. He's not so bad. Nice little critter. He's trying to learn. He's...wait one minute! That window is chest high! How can he be looking out? I stared at him. He looked so pleased. His black eyes sparkled happily from between the curtains. Then, it hit me. The kitchen table was in front of the window!

I charged into the house. There he was, perched on the table, wagging his tail at me! How can such a little dog get up so high! Blast it! I plopped him on the floor, and his route upward became apparent as he enthusiastically hopped up onto a chair, then scurried onto the table. I guess he wanted me to compliment his climbing ability. It seemed Frosty had aspirations to be a mountain goat.

From then on, whenever we left the house, we tipped the four kitchen chairs inward so he couldn't climb upward. Another victory for me! Or so I thought. That worked as long as we didn't forget about the chairs. When we did, we always found him happily sitting or lying on the table. Yuck! Dog butt on my table!

Remember the statement, "If I do a good job, and I will, having a dog won't impact our lives in any way?" Do you remember that ridiculous statement?

Let's assess the "won't impact" part. We put a door where we didn't want one. I gave up my storage cubbyhole. Whenever we left, we had to tip all kitchen chairs inward. My fuzzy slippers were stiff with spit. We had holes in our yard. When I visited my Mom and had Frosty along, we had to sit in the kitchen. I was forced to put all shoes in the closet and keep the door shut. My plant no longer proudly sat on the floor in its fancy pot. Then, there's the issue of keeping doors closed and feeling claustrophobic. Oh, sure, Frosty wasn't impacting our lives in any way.

Let's move on and address the issue of having a living "intruder barking alarm." Frosty was proficient at barking. He was loud for such a little dog, and persistent too. He would bark and bark and bark. I would run to the door to see who was trying to break in. Hmmm. No one's there. What's he barking at? He probably chased the bad guys away.

He barked and barked. I ran to the window and peered out. Hmm. No one's there, either. What's he barking at? Probably kids that he scared off.

He barked and barked. I ran to the back door. No one's there, either! No one's anywhere! What the blazes is he barking at?

He barked and barked. I listened carefully. The only sound, other than Frosty yapping, was some child on a bike across the street. Uh-oh. We might have a glitch in the intruder barking alarm. Could it be that he barks at every sound? Oh, yes. Every sound. Leaves scraping across the sidewalk. Children playing. Laughing adults. Passing cars. The wind.

At this point, it became apparent that Frosty was an inefficient alarm system. He went off, unnecessarily, much too often. (Exactly like our present car alarm.) So, I disconnected him from my reality.

The next time he barked and barked and barked, I didn't bother to get up or look. I developed a new strategy. It was called, "Frosty! Quiet!"

I either completely ignored his barking or shouted, "Frosty! Quiet!" Jack the Ripper could have been peering in the window, and I would have been yelling, "Frosty! Quiet!" That cuddly pile of white fur lived to be 16 years old. If I had a dollar for every time he barked and I yelled, "Frosty! Quiet!" I would be a trillionaire!

On a routine trip to Dr. Vet, I noticed an obedience class ad on the bulletin board. At the time, I had Frosty on the end of a leash. He was leaping and barking at a kitty in a cage. I deplored that behavior, but couldn't seem to get him to stop. I mentally made a list of Frosty's obnoxious behaviors. It went like this. Walking Frosty was always frustrating. He loved to be out in front even though he was gasping for air because of the collar. He had an obnoxious habit of jumping on people. He didn't come when called. He didn't do a lot of things. I decided I might be deficient in the training department. So, I wrote down the phone number, and when I got home, called and enrolled in the class. I thought, This will be a piece of cake with a professional trainer in charge. I'll sit back and watch this dog be trained. Sounds like a brilliant plan to me!

I'll never forget that first lesson. Mr. Dog Trainer paced back and forth in front of a group of doggy malcontents who were yapping at each other and struggling against leashes. Frosty might have been the smallest, but he was right up there with the most obnoxious and loudest. Mr. Dog Trainer stopped in front of me. I thought, proudly, He's going to admire my cute little dog.

Mr. Trainer scowled and said, disdainfully, "Even little dogs need to be trained. Especially this one."

I thought, Oh really? Could it be that's why we're here? If he were trained, I wouldn't need you! And I resent your tone!

Mr. Trainer then informed us that he was not going to train the dogs, he was going to teach us to train our dogs. Excuse me? Teach...us? Hold on! I thought I was going to watch, and Frosty was going to be trained. The ad didn't say anything about me being involved. Hmm. Is this a good idea? Of course it is. I mean, how hard can dog training be? It might even be fun.

Mr. Trainer's eyes roved over the mostly male class, then rested on me. He said, slightly disgustedly, "Women do not make very good dog trainers. They're too soft. They say, (at this point he raised his voice several octaves and said in a wimpy tone), 'No, Duke, no.' He lowered his voice and said, "Men know how to say no." He barked, loudly, "Duke, no!"

Even though everyone in the building winced, including the dogs, I, for one, wasn't particularly impressed. I grew up with three brothers, six uncles, and a streetwise, cussing Dad. Loud masculine voices, even loud, threatening masculine voices, did not intimidate me in any way. I had learned at any early age to ignore all the ranting, raving, and posturing. I thought, Back off, buster! I'll show you. Anything you can teach, I can learn!

Mr. Trainer went on to point out that dogs consider women their "mothers" and men their "masters." Then, he suggested I let my husband train the dog.

Excuse me! Men—masters?

I said, "I'm training Frosty." I was thinking, We'll see who's "mother" and who's "master." I'll show you.

That "I'll show you" thing has gotten me in so much trouble throughout my life, I'm not even going to attempt to make a list.

Mr. Trainer gave us our first lesson. I took the knowledge home and worked with Frosty three times a day for a week. And, let me tell you, at the end of that time and in that class, Frosty showed his stuff. I said, "Frosty, sit!" in my deepest voice, and he proudly did exactly that. Of course, when he stood, he leaped to the end of his leash and barked frantically at the dog next to us, but I was undaunted. Frosty had sat. On command. That other stuff was too advanced for us. I thought, We're brilliant! What's next? We're ready to move on to the tough stuff.

We confidently went on to "down." Down proved to be harder. Frosty was energetic. He didn't understand why he had to lay down in the middle of the floor when there were things to chase and exploring to do. "Because I said so" didn't seem to compute. However, I had a point to make. That being, this female could and would train that dog. I worked that little Westie every day. Three times a day we went up and down the sidewalk. He sat. He downed. He sat. He downed. He sat. He downed. We were awesome!

The class went on to "heeling." Here, we ran into a few minor problems. Frosty was supposed to walk at my side with the leash loose. He didn't quite grasp the concept of "heeling." He was bred to chase critters. In his mind, a critter was anything that was moving in front, beside, or in back of him. And, his instinct was to bark in hot pursuit as he strained at the leash. Walking at my side and listening to orders was not in his game plan.

In those days, trainers used choke collars and the "jerk" method. It seemed Frosty, even though he was a half-pint, had the mindset and determination of a Saint Bernard. So, I was shown how to jerk the leash to get Frosty under control. It worked. Sort of. The method was unreliable because success was determined by Frosty's mood and determination level. I worked on "heeling" and worked on "heeling" and worked on "heeling." I might not be the world's smartest dog trainer, but I am no quitter. Maybe the "no quitter" part was the problem. Quitting might have been the smartest thing to do.

After many classes, Frosty and I came to an agreement. He would "heel" in obedience class if I didn't insist he "heel" outside. I figured what the trainer didn't know wouldn't hurt him, Frosty, or me. We were fairly successful in class. At the end of class, I hurried out of the building and put Frosty in the car. Fast! One advantage of having small dogs is—if all else fails, pick them up and carry them!

By obedience class graduation, we were a splendid team. We could sit, down, heel, do the recall on lead, stand for examination (sort of), and do a long sit and down (all on a leash.) I was really getting into the training thing and decided to go into the advanced class. Maybe I could enter Frosty in an obedience show. I liked working with him at home and enjoyed the classes, so I enrolled in the advanced course.

You know when you look back at your life and identify the turning points? The defining moments? The bad decisions? The going down the wrong path? Enrolling in the advanced class may have been one of those.

I hung on Mr. Trainer's every word and suggestion. He knew his stuff. But, I will resent for eternity the night he told me Frosty was smarter than me and we were having problems because the dog was out thinking me. Even though Mr. Trainer may have been—and I stress may have been—correct, I don't think it's proper etiquette to sneer into a struggling woman's face that her midget dog is smarter than she! Be that as it may, I was not to be discouraged by a half-pint dog or an instructor who obviously didn't recognize exceptional dog-trainer talent when it stood before his eyes!

And, besides, no canine is smarter than me! However, Mr. Trainer proved his point in an odd way. Actually, my super intelligent dog decided to help him. Mr. Trainer was lecturing us about training dogs to obey commands when off their leashes. He stated that some dogs consistently run away when let off the leash. I thought, disgustedly, Even I know all dogs run away if they get the chance. No way am I going to trust this white munchkin without a leash attached to my hand! Mr. Trainer said running off and not coming when called were not acceptable behaviors and downright dangerous if a car was involved.

My technique up to now had been to eliminate the chances of running away by keeping Frosty on a leash or tied up. The concept of letting him run loose filled me with dread. He had escaped a few times, and I called, "Frosty, come" until I was blue in the face. Guess what? He didn't come. I either had to trick him, outmaneuver him, or follow him through the neighborhood waiting for him to either stop to be petted by someone or collapse from exhaustion.

Mr. Trainer was confident we could teach our dogs to stay by our sides and come when called. I thought, Hah! What dimension are you living in?

As Mr. Trainer droned on about "off leash," I'm thinking, Oh no! This guy is serious!

He took a short, thick chain (about 12″ long) and tossed it up and down in his hand. He explained it was called a "throw chain." He said we were to heel our dogs off leash. When they bolted, he'd throw the chain at their feet. Not at the dogs, but close. The chain made a zinging sound when it was airborne and a loud noise when it smacked against the concrete. Dogs would always flee from the sound and head for safety and security. That safety and security would be their owners. We were to call them and praise them when they came scurrying back. Mr. Trainer confidently said he'd never had a dog that didn't flee back to its owner when the chain did its zinging noise against concrete things.

Okay. I'm game. It seems logical.

We took turns. First, the big black Labrador. He looked so happy bolting from his owner. Mr. Trainer tossed the chain and, sure enough, when it sailed through the air, the Labrador's ears went up and when the chain smacked against the concrete at his feet, the Labrador went fleeing back to his owner who praised him so much it was nauseating.

I watched several other dogs go through the same process. Mr. Trainer was correct. They all scurried back to their handlers. I looked down at Frosty to see if he was frightened by all the noise and upset dogs. The other dogs looked a tad fearful from the commotion. I didn't want my little fellow to be worried. Animals sense fear. Poor Frosty's probably frightened. He's probably telepathic and picking up on the bad vibes. He's probably...wait one moment! That is not a fear posture!

Frosty's full attention was on the proceedings. He wasn't however, worried or fearful. His tail was wagging a mile a minute, his black eyes were sparkling, and he had that big Westie grin on. I'm thinking, Why do I just know this is not going to end up the way Mr. Trainer thinks it will.

I swear it was like Frosty was memorizing what was going on, assessing the outcome, getting a strategy ready, and making his own action plan.

It was finally our turn. We were always last. Maybe because Frosty was so small and seemed insignificant somehow. I took Frosty's leash off, stepped forward, and said, "Frosty, heel!"

Frosty started off with me, then decided he wanted to play with the black Labrador. Frosty bolted, his little feet slipping and sliding on the concrete floor. Mr. Trainer threw the chain into the air so it would fall at Frosty's feet. It zinged, then banged on the concrete. Frosty stopped in his tracks, studied Mr. Trainer a moment, glanced at me, calmly pranced over to the chain, picked it up in his little teeth, and dragged it to Mr. Trainer. I guess Frosty thought it was a fetch game and the other dogs were too stupid to realize Mr. Trainer wanted it back. After all, each time after their dogs scurried to them, the handlers retrieved the chain and gave it back to Mr. Trainer. Obviously, Frosty decided to skip the middleman and help out Mr. Trainer. My darling Westie was glad to be of service. And, that chain was heavy, so dragging it across the floor was no easy task.

I will remember the shocked look on Mr. Trainer's face until the day I die.

Training Frosty to heel off leash took a great deal of work and, even though he eventually stayed with me and came when called, I never fully trusted him and his Terrier instincts. I always carefully chose when and where he was loose.

I eagerly looked forward to our once-a-week training sessions. As frustrating as they were, I realized I loved working with that obstinate little Westie. After teaching us the basics, Mr. Trainer began readying us to show in obedience trials.

Our class moved on to the figure eight. The figure eight consisted of two human posts that stood several feet apart. The dog and owner stood between the human posts. The judge (or instructor) said, "Forward." You moved forward and around the first post. The idea was that your dog walked right next to you in spite of the turns and change of position. As you walked around the posts, you made a figure eight. The instructor said, "Halt." You stopped. Then he said, "Forward," and you continued your trek around the posts, still making the figure eight. You did not want the dog to swing away from you when he was on the outside or crowd you when he was on the inside.

The recall was a bit frustrating. You left your dog, told him to wait, crossed the room, and when the instructor cued you, you called the dog. He was supposed to run straight to you and immediately sit in front of you. I have a question. How could a dog, who moved at the speed of sound, slow his walk down to barely an amble when called? I would call Frosty. He would dejectedly trudge along with his ears down, glaring at Mr. Trainer, then would slowly sit in front of me with a huge chip on his shoulder.

The stand for examination was also a challenge. When told to "stand," the dog was supposed to stand still while the instructor went over his body, touching his head, shoulders, and hips. You must admit, it is hard to stand still when you're wagging your tail, and entire body, as a person approaches. Maybe, if you sniggle and wiggle hard enough, he'll change his mind and decide to tell you what a swell guy you are and pet you. Maybe, if you just walk up to him, he'll smile and admire you. And, if he won't, who cares, you'll find someone who does. Of course, that means walking away from the ridiculous and obviously prejudiced-against-Westies instructor. That did blow the stand for examination part of the exercise. But, that didn't seem to bother Frosty, who always found someone in the class to admire him.

Mr. Trainer encouraged us to enter our dogs in an upcoming obedience trial "fun match" where scores and trophies would be awarded. He suggested the pre-novice class. In those days, it consisted of heeling, the figure eight, stand for examination, recall, and long sit and down, all on leash. Fun matches were held as practice for AKC shows where points were awarded toward conformation championships and obedience titles. The matches could consist of conformation entries only, obedience entries only, or a combination of both. Matches were a "fun" way to learn and practice.

Frosty was working fairly consistently on leash, so I was tempted. Mr. Trainer and his wife, who helped out at lessons, were encouraging me to give it a try. In a rash moment of confidence I decided, Okay! I can do it!

I entered that fun match and it changed my life forever.

At that point, Mrs. Trainer tactfully suggested that Frosty needed grooming. I remember looking down at him and thinking, What does she mean? I've been brushing him.

True, he was scruffy looking, with white hair popping askew all over, but that was part of his persona. And true, the hair did cover his eyes in places, but I thought that was how it was supposed to be. And, also true, his white coat wasn't exactly white anymore, but I thought, maybe Westies turned gray as they aged.

This delightful woman said if I was going to show him, I better consider taking him to a grooming shop. I asked, "What's a grooming shop? Do you shop for 'grooms' there?" I don't need a groom. I have a husband, but come to think about it, if I had known there was a place to shop for "grooms," maybe I could have done better.

She laughed and said I had a delightful sense of humor. I didn't have the heart to tell her I wasn't joking. The whole premise of shopping for a groom definitely had appeal.

She went on to explain that a grooming shop was a place where dedicated people turned scruffy dogs beautiful, much like a beauty salon. She also gently lectured that responsible dog owners needed to realize their canine companions were entitled to proper grooming.

I could see her point about brushing, bathing, and cutting toenails, but it seemed silly to me that Frosty needed a doggie hairstylist. But, I loved the little critter, and if Mr. and Mrs. Trainer thought he needed a makeover, I would find a doggie beauty parlor. I turned to the phone book and, sure enough, there was such a place. I made an appointment, and when I picked Frosty up after his session, I couldn't believe my eyes. He was white, trimmed, and one handsome little dude, complete with a bow tied between his ears.

We were now ready for our debut.

The day of Frosty's fun match came. It was a gorgeous autumn day in Wisconsin. The trees were red and gold and swayed under a delicate, warm breeze. There were white, cottony clouds slowly floating across blue sky. The weather was perfect and nourished your soul.

The match was held at a local park. My children went to Granny's for the day. Bruce, Frosty, and I pulled onto the parking lot and I fought sheer panic. There were several rings set up for participants. The park was filled with dogs and people who appeared to know what they were doing. I was not one of those confident people.

I wanted to go home. Immediately! Forget this fun match stuff!

Bruce, who has always been at my side encouraging me to finish what I start, gently told me I could do this. He had watched me practice, and he was sure. I think I actually offended Bruce in several prior lives and the Universe is getting even with me and evening out karma by having Bruce encourage my ridiculous antics so everyone gets a jolly laugh. Come to think about it, I probably have offended the entire Universe and most souls in prior lives.

Bruce is patient, loving, and confident in my ability, even when I am not. I was not totally convinced I should go through with this trip into insanity. We spent an hour watching people go through various obedience routines. It was pretty obvious that the pre-novices, like myself, weren't exactly polished. The class I had entered was done entirely on leash, so at least I didn't have to worry about chasing Frosty as he galloped down the highway. I shyly went to the steward's table and picked up the armband displaying my number. I was shaking so hard Bruce had to help me put it on around my upper arm.

As each dog was put through the sequence of heeling, figure eight, stand for examination, and recall, my nervousness lessened. They were all beginners, just like me, and not perfect in any way. Bruce and I chuckled when a huge chocolate Labrador lifted his leg on his owner after he recalled impressively. The critter decided he needed to empty himself between sitting in front of his owner and the by-heel, which meant the dog returned to the heeling position. Almost every dog made mistakes and most of those mistakes were very funny. Here is a lesson for you to remember. Never laugh at anyone in the position that you will soon be in yourself. The Universe has a way of reprimanding individuals dumb enough to laugh at others.

Our turn came. I managed to get into the ring without fainting from nervousness. There I stood in front of a real judge, with Frosty sitting by my side. The judge said, "Forward!" And, forward we went. The judge said, "Halt!" I halted. Frosty kept going. At least, until he ran out of leash. The dogs were supposed to sit when you stopped. Frosty had other things on his mind. He may have "goofed up," but he did it with confidence and flair! He loved all the goings on at that "fun" match. I'm glad he was having fun. I was not. I decided that the word "fun" was a huge misnomer and the matches needed to be renamed with something like "confidence shattering matches" or "destroy your ego matches."

Frosty turned to me and wagged his tail happily. I could read his eyes. They said, "Thanks for bringing me to this fun place, Mom!"

The judge said, "Forward!" Away we went. He said, "Halt!" I halted again. Frosty stood, wagged, and checked out the audience. I turned left. Frosty bounded this way and that. I turned right. Frosty hopped along, black eyes sparkling. Walk didn't seem to be in his vocabulary that day.

Guess what. We flunked.

Next was the figure eight. Now, I admit I was a bit flustered and thinking about fleeing the ring and may not have been properly focused. The judge said, "Forward!" Around the human posts we went. He said, "Halt." We halted and Frosty actually sat. I was getting confident. We went through the entire routine without a flaw.

I smiled inwardly, thinking, I can do this stuff! I am one awesome trainer. We flunked heeling, but we were very impressive on the figure eight.

We went on to the stand for examination. Frosty stood, but then walked to the judge, wagging at him and wriggling happily while he was being examined. We flunked, but Frosty made friends with the judge.

We went on to recall. Frosty was only a leash length in front of me, avoiding eye contact with me, and smiling his Westie grin at the judge. I said, "Frosty, come!" Remember, this is the dog who was hopping happily when heeling and who walked up to the judge on the stand. You'd think he'd at least stand up. Nope. Didn't. Just sat there smiling. At least I wasn't embarrassed by his slow, belligerent ambling.

We flunked.

Even though we flunked heeling, stand, and recall, I was giddy with happiness when we left the ring. Okay, Frosty made a fool out of me on those exercises, but I had mastered the figure eight!

I noticed people smiling and laughing and thought they were admiring Frosty's one accomplishment. I walked up to Bruce and smiled proudly. He was smiling too. He said we did an excellent job. He was proud, even though Frosty, obviously, needed some more lessons. But, Bruce had a question. He managed not to smirk when he asked, "Why did you keep going around the same person on the figure eight? Isn't it supposed to be a figure eight? Doesn't that mean going around both people?"

I was indignant. I replied, "I did not go around the same person twice. That would be two circles. I know I did a figure eight!"

Bruce just shook his head. Nope. I had done circles. Now I knew why everyone was smiling and laughing.

We flunked figure eight! My best thing! And the judge's notation on the score sheet under figure eight? Handler error. Wait one moment! That dratted dog fouls up over and over again, and I get reprimanded for making one tiny mistake? That seemed unfair to me.

Frosty stood on the long down and laid down on the long sit. I think we probably had the lowest score ever given out at an obedience "fun" match. His total score was 34 out of 160. After all these years, I still remember that score. It's emblazoned in my memory.

I vowed never to return to the ring. Too bad I don't keep my vows. It would have saved wear and tear on my nerves! In a match a few months later, Frosty improved to 57. Wow! Then, in the next match, he actually made 86. It's amazing I can still remember those scores. I can't remember how old my children are, but I know those scores. Let's see. At that rate, how old would Frosty be before we can trust him off leash and he gets his obedience title? And, for that matter, how old will I be? It might be hard to wobble around the ring at age 142.

Frosty got that obedience title years later. But, that's a different story and involves plotting, manipulation, outsmarting my daughter Sheri and me, weeks of training, and perseverance like you wouldn't believe. However, we Boettchers never give up and are not quitters! For your information...neither are Terriers. And it helps if the Terrier (Frosty) and the trainers (Kathy and Sheri) are on the same page as to goals, future dreams, etc. If not? Oh, well, trying is supposed to be what makes all endeavors fun.

I pouted for several days after my first "fun" match ordeal. I lamented that I was a dog training failure. Then, one night in bed, I changed my vow from "never to return" to "I am going to do this!" No dog is going to defeat me!

We returned to dog training class, Frosty with his tail high in the air and wagging enthusiastically, me with my tail tucked between my legs.

Mr. Trainer tactfully suggested perhaps I was "overtraining" and that's why Frosty had fouled up so badly. Overtraining? What does that mean? How can you "overtrain?" I thought working Frosty's little tush off with three training sessions a day was a good thing. I thought being a motivated, dedicated trainer with a steadfast routine would reap results. Of course, my "fun" match didn't exactly reap positive results and it sure wasn't "fun."

I scowled as I was told that Frosty, obviously, knew everything I was working on, but was probably bored by doing the same routine over and over again. Boredom leads to lethargy or creativity. Frosty chose creativity. That being, "Let's have fun with Mom! Let's play with her head! Let's liven up this boring routine that makes no sense. Why bother doing the same dumb thing over and over again? I can make some new friends at this fun match and do things in a more exciting way!"

Oh, come on now. He's a twerp of a dog. Surely, he can't be that smart and wouldn't.... Why is Frosty grinning that impish Westie smile? Have I been outwitted and used for amusement by that fur pile?

Mr. Trainer thought the whole thing was pretty funny and lectured that I needed to get more creative and make training challenging for Frosty. Hold the phone! It's challenging for me, now I have to make it challenging for that critter? Isn't he supposed to do what I say, when I say it, because I'm the trainer and boss and he's the trainee? No one told me I was going to have to work at training. I thought it just happened if you kept repeating the lesson. No such luck. Apparently, you have to "interact and challenge," not just instruct.

Oh, dear. This might be a trifle more complicated than I thought. Should I just let it all go and have a dog that has no manners and doesn't listen? I admit it was tempting. I could just let him jump on people, run away, and tug me down the street. In the overall picture of life, does this stuff matter?

I sighed despondently. Of course it mattered. I didn't want him running away and getting hit by a car or lost because he wouldn't stay with me or come when I called. Jumping on people is just plain discourteous. And, he gasped for air when he leaned into the collar. That couldn't be good for him. After pondering my dilemma, I concluded I was going to have to innovatively train, even if it was work. After all, the original goal was to teach Frosty manners. And, the truth was, he had improved. Maybe I could teach him to do "fun" match if I tried some new methods. Why not quit after you acquire manners and skip the fun match thing? Good question. If I ever figure out the answer to that, I'll get back to you.

Okay, back to the drawing board. Put aside your ego and suck it up.

I started training every other day and began varying the routine by doing unexpected things. That meant Frosty had to concentrate harder and he had less "head" room to be creative. Once again, we began to improve.

About this time, I decided it was costing too much to have Frosty groomed. I looked him over and thought, I bet I could do this. How hard can it be? There's that ridiculous statement again. You would think I had learned by now that many "simple" looking things require hard work to make them look "simple." Are you following that? I hope so, because my lack of understanding of that principle has led to many ridiculous situations.

After talking with people at dog training class, I discovered there were schools that taught dog grooming. I decided I could not only save money by grooming Frosty, I might actually be able to earn money grooming other dogs. So, I found a class in the newspaper and signed up.

I was a little put off when I discovered the class was being held in some gal's basement. I expected a school complete with classrooms, lockers, and corridors, not a dungeon. But, she seemed to know her stuff. She was actually quite an entrepreneur. Not only did she earn money teaching people how to groom dogs in her dog grooming school, she was making money on the dogs her students groomed. You see, she also had a dog grooming salon business. Those doggie customers were used in her classes. Her students did the grooming for her customers and she was paid by students and customers for grooming the same dog. Clever? I thought so, even though I resented being used that way. However, I got over the resentment. I wanted to learn.

There was one glitch. I needed to learn to groom Westies. She groomed poodles. In the beginning, I didn't realize there were different methods required for different breeds. I thought grooming was simply "grooming." It never occurred to me that, if that were the case, all breeds' coiffures would look alike. So, I spent seven weeks learning to groom poodles thinking I could apply the techniques to my Westie. I really enjoyed those classes. I grew to love the poodles' temperament, and it was fun turning grungy little critters into beasts of beauty.

Just before the last lesson, I suddenly realized I didn't want Frosty to look like a poodle with a cute topknot and puffy tail. So, I decided to take him with me for a lesson in Westie hairdos. After all, when I originally signed up, Ms. Grooming Instructor had assured me she could teach me to groom my Westie.

When I arrived with Frosty tucked under my arm, Ms. Grooming Instructor seemed annoyed. She dragged out a book, showed me several pictures of the steps necessary to groom a Westie, and suggested I buy it. She told me his face needed to be shaped like a plate, that his pads should not be shaved like a poodle foot, to clip his body with a "five" blade, clean his ears, shape his body with a scissors, and leave a few furnishings. End of lesson.

I imagine you Terrier people are cringing. Clip a Westie? Clip a Terrier? NO, stop! They are supposed to be hand stripped, not clipped! But, Ms. Grooming Instructor failed to mention that fact. And, the grooming shop to which I had been taking Frosty clipped his coat, so I didn't question that suggestion. I took the clipper and buzzed over his coat. I must brag here that Frosty looked pretty sharp when I finished with him. He didn't actually resemble a properly groomed Westie, but he didn't look like a poodle, so I guess that was an accomplishment in itself.

I decided to sell my new poodle grooming skills. I set up my own grooming salon in my basement and spent the next two years grooming poodles and Frosty. I loved doing it. I didn't make much money, but I enjoyed working with my doggie clients.

About that time, someone in my dog training class suggested that I should consider showing Frosty in breed conformation at AKC dog shows. That notion intrigued me, so I found a Westie breeder through Mr. Dog Trainer and asked if I could bring Frosty over for a critique. She agreed. The next day, we were in another basement filled with dog crates and grooming tables.

The woman visibly winced when I proudly put Frosty on the table. She was straightforward and said I would never be able to show Frosty in breed conformation, because he had been neutered. Altered males and females were not allowed to compete.

Hmmm. That seemed unfair to me. Frosty couldn't help that he was only given one and a smidgen, and that they were taken away. But, oh well. If that's the rule, our conformation show career was over.

Then, she went on to say that even if he hadn't been neutered, he had a terrible overbite that was considered a serious fault in a Westie. In her opinion, that alone should have kept Frosty out of conformation competition and from being used as a stud. I knew about the "bite" thing from Dr. Vet and it made sense. But, I know people with overbites and no one disqualifies them from breeding. Of course, if you're neutered, I suppose the point is moot.

Then, she said his body was too long, his head too long, and his legs too short.

Excuse me! Now we're getting personal and insulting! I thought her face was a bit long and her legs a tad short too, but I wasn't going on and on and on about those things.

Actually, the woman was blunt, but not unkind. I learned a great deal about conformation from her in those few hours. She taught me that beauty is in the eye of the beholder, unless you're planning on competing in breed conformation. Then, it's in the eye of the judge who has a physical and temperament AKC breed standard against which to compare your animal.

She taught me that if you decide to breed animals, it needs to be done with the knowledge to improve your dogs' offspring. Responsible breeders strive to eliminate faults. And you can't eliminate faults if you don't recognize them. If you don't want to take the time to educate yourself about the science and art of breeding, your animal should be neutered. There's a great deal of responsibility that goes with breeding, including finding proper homes for puppies. You see the results of irresponsible breeding every time you visit Humane Societies and animal shelters.

Dogs that are not breeding stock still make wonderful pets. And, that's exactly what Frosty was—a wonderful, neutered pet.

And, even though I thought Frosty was the most beautiful, perfect Westie alive, when the breeder took the time to compare him to several of her champions, even a novice like me could see the differences. It didn't change the way I felt about Frosty. However, the differences were obvious and it became apparent why Frosty's faults would put him at a disadvantage if he were being utilized for chasing varmints.

I came away from that visit with a whole new perspective. I took Frosty back to obedience class and started looking at the dogs in class in an entirely different way. I bought books about dog structure and gait. I applied my new knowledge to every dog I saw and began to recognize good structure from bad. I bought *The American Kennel Club's Complete Dog Book* and studied the conformation of every breed. I imagined what it would be like to compete with a perfect specimen in breed conformation, as well as obedience competition.

I didn't know it at the time, but I had been bitten by the dreaded "showing" bug. And, that bite can change your life forever. Just ask any of the people you see at dog shows. You can easily recognize them. They are the ones rushing from one ring to another with a dog in tow, an armband on, a frantic look in their eyes, and a motor vehicle that is bought to accommodate animals. You can bet they have a home that is set up for the convenience of raising dogs. Do I seem knowledgeable? That's because I am. I have traveled that road and loved every moment.

However, at this particular time, even though I was gaining knowledge about all the dog breeds, I was just trying to get Frosty to a point where we could acquire an obedience title. I wanted him to have manners, but the competitive side of me really wanted that obedience title. I loved that obstinate Westie with all my heart. He brought joy into our lives every day and continued to do that for years. I admired his courage and independence. Imagine being that small and having no fear. That's to be admired. At that time, there was a school of thought that said dogs should be forced to obey. If breaking their spirit was part of the process, then so be it. I just could not buy in to that philosophy. I didn't want to change Frosty's personality or take away his spirit of adventure. I wanted to work with him and train him to understand that, when I gave an order, it had to be followed. Breaking his spirit or changing him was never an option for me.

I decided that Mr. Dog Trainer was correct. Frosty knew the commands and was toying with me. I was the one who needed to be better educated in how to best communicate with the white furry critter. Our progress was slow and we kept working as the months passed. But, there was progress and I relished each and every achievement. When I called, "Frosty, come!" and he actually came, I was thrilled to death!

I had pondered getting another Westie for showing in conformation, but now knew that the dog had to be hand stripped and I wasn't sure I wanted to do that. The breeder had shown me the technique and explained the work involved in showing a Westie in conformation. The time she took with me gave me the facts and for that I'll always be grateful. I would come to learn that conscientious breeders never mind spending time with people who want to acquire their breed. They want to educate you about the drawbacks of their favorite dogs, as well as the up side. If you want to know the truth about a breed, talk to a reputable breeder. They won't hold anything back. They'll also be honest about genetic defects, guarantee the health of the puppy, and explain the disadvantages, as well as advantages, of having their breed.

Luscious green summer was giving way to another colorful autumn in Wisconsin. Leaves of red, orange, and rust decorated the trees and the fresh, evening air had a bit of nip to it. Frosty and I were still faithfully attending our obedience classes. He was now two-years-old. When I was in class, I was filled with confidence. I could see Frosty improving. I was, however, a realist (not a coward) and knew in my heart that succeeding in class and competing in the obedience ring were very different endeavors. Having had my ego destroyed three times in pre-novice trials, I opted for the enthusiasm borne of classes and stayed away from "fun" matches of any kind.

Chapter Two

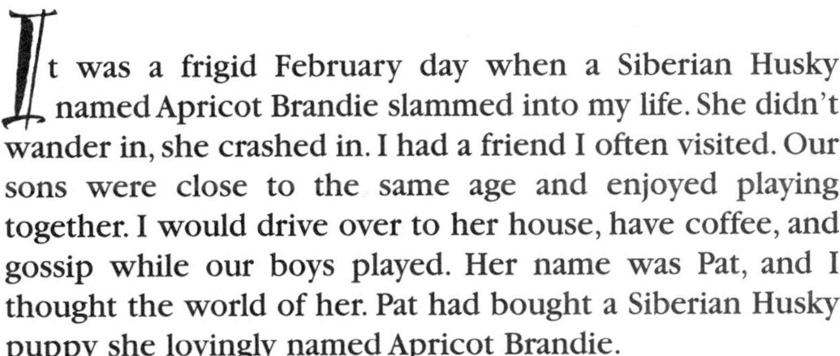

It was a frigid February day when a Siberian Husky named Apricot Brandie slammed into my life. She didn't wander in, she crashed in. I had a friend I often visited. Our sons were close to the same age and enjoyed playing together. I would drive over to her house, have coffee, and gossip while our boys played. Her name was Pat, and I thought the world of her. Pat had bought a Siberian Husky puppy she lovingly named Apricot Brandie.

Brandie adored me from the moment she laid eyes on me. She was now two-years-old, had dancing, playful eyes, and possessed an amazing energy level. Brandie was gray and white with a touch of apricot color across her shoulders. Her mischievous brown eyes sparkled and her tail never stopped wagging. She always greeted me with spirited body slams and wet loving kisses.

As winter turned to spring, Brandie and I became close friends. She seemed to encourage my spirit to be free of all "normalcy."

When I visited Pat, Brandie was always thrilled to see me and I glowed inside at every zealous greeting. My ego thought Brandie considered me a "special" person. What I came to understand much later is that Siberian Huskies, as a breed, are always glad to see everyone. They consider humanity put on this Earth so that they can enthusiastically romp with them, lick their faces, lovingly knock them over, and have someone to chase them when they escape, which can happen fairly often. Incidentally, the "escape" thing is what was driving my friend's husband to insanity.

Brandie escaped almost daily and loved to run through the neighborhood with Pat or her husband, Don, hot on her heels. Don was becoming more and more frustrated with Brandie's antics. He finally stopped chasing her and decided if she didn't come back, he really didn't care. I think he was hoping she would disappear forever. However, Brandie always found her way home. I didn't know it at the time, but Siberians are bred to run and that's what they'll do at every opportunity.

Brandie was also turning Don's yard into a field of deep holes. Don was convinced she was trying to dig her way to Siberia. I thought maybe she was digging a den. The interesting thing was—there was never any leftover dirt. Lots of holes, no piles of dirt. Don snapped at me one day, as I tried to figure out why she was digging. He didn't care why she was digging, he just wanted her to stop!

While Brandie and Don's relationship steadily deteriorated, I decided Don probably wasn't treating her well enough for her to want to hang around, because she was still touring the neighborhood every day. Now, I should have known better than to make that assumption. After all, I treated Frosty like royalty, and he took off to explore whenever he got the chance. He loved our neighbor's rabbit hutch and always headed across the street straight for their yard with me right behind. I guess he considered the rabbits as close to a "rodent" as he would ever get. So, what was so different in my situation than Don's? I know. Brandie was bigger and covered ground faster, so his task of capture was more difficult. However, anyone who has given chase to a Westie on the lookout for prey will tell you they can cover ground at an amazing pace.

Back to Brandie and Don. Brandie's list of antics was growing. Added to the list was her habit of piddling at his feet and on his feet—a submissive behavior, but annoying nonetheless. At least, it's generally thought that type of behavior is submissive. I wasn't so sure. I thought, maybe Brandie was trying to tell Don what she thought of him.

Brandie also decided to challenge his leadership by jumping onto the sofa and growling when he tried to sit down. Apparently she wanted to be leader of their pack. Then, Brandie decided to become a gourmet and began sampling bread and cheese whenever it was left on the kitchen counter. Don caught her with a cheese brick wedged sideways in her mouth. He didn't think her jack-o-lantern grin was funny, especially when he tried to pry out the cheese and got a nasty growl.

The final straw came in April when Don, who was carrying several bags of groceries, stepped into a cavern that Brandie had just dug. Don always skillfully avoided holes, but she blindsided him with a freshly dug one. Perhaps I should clarify something here. Siberians do not actually dig holes. They dig CANYONS! Don, who thought he had the location of all her holes memorized, confidently stepped around an old hole and into the new ravine that ran through his yard. Groceries flew in all directions. Don twisted his ankle and bit the dust. I won't repeat the words he used when he took after Brandie at a wobble. I know what they were, because his three-year-old son repeated them to me. Leave it to a child to learn that which should be left unlearned.

When I visited the next day, I found Pat in tears. Don was going to take Brandie to the Humane Society. He refused to deal with the Siberian anymore. In his defense, their yard did look like a military exercise had taken place under a barrage of mortar fire, his foot was wet with fresh piddle, he had just wiped up the floor again, his ankle was wrapped, and he was painfully limping, limiting his ability to chase after Brandie, who had made off with another loaf of bread.

I looked into Brandie's brown eyes and could not imagine letting this free spirit go to the dog pound. This time, I failed to heed my research and just went with my heart. I realized I had fallen in love with this rambunctious, incorrigible Siberian Husky.

I went home, thought it over, and decided, in my lunacy, that a second dog would be a good thing. Frosty would have a playmate. I could keep Brandie tied in the yard, and I would enroll her in the obedience class that took place right after Frosty's. Think of that! I could do two obedience classes in one night and have two dogs to work with at home. That way, I wouldn't "over train" Frosty. Brandie would be fun to train. Surely, such a beautiful, obviously intelligent Siberian could be easily trained. (I mean, after all, she always found her way home. She had to be smart.) And, I could show Brandie at obedience trial fun matches. She couldn't possibly be as uncooperative as Frosty when he was in a Terrier snit.

Little did I know that Brandie's agenda was to train her humans, not be trained. Actually, that wasn't any different than Frosty's agenda.

Remember all the parameters I put on getting a first dog? Size, trainability, etc? I ask you, why did I just throw all that away in making my decision this time? But, I guess that's what love does. It takes away your ability to reason!

Bruce reluctantly agreed to let me bring Brandie home. At this point, I had an inspiration. Don was disgusted and defeated because he was always chasing Brandie. Don wasn't stupid. He diligently tied her up. But, she always managed to get loose. When she slept in their house, she was proficient at slipping past anyone who opened a door. So, I decided that we would put a small kennel behind our house. That way, Brandie would not have to be tied, and she would be contained. In addition, if we poured a concrete slab, she couldn't dig holes and get out under the kennel fence. That meant she would never escape. There is a flaw in that theory, but we'll get to it later.

I told Don and Pat I would take Brandie if they would keep her until the kennel was ready. They agreed.

Bruce has a kind, generous uncle who was a mason. He took over the concrete pouring part of the project. Bruce helped Bob dig out the area for the slab, and Bob engineered the concrete flooring. The kennel would be 6´x 12´. Once the concrete hardened, we added a chain link kennel, and Brandie's new home was almost ready. I purchased the largest doghouse I could find in the JC Penney catalog. It looked simple enough to put together. I mean, how hard can it be to assemble a basic doghouse? It's just sides, a floor, a roof, and a door.

The doghouse arrived. I thought, How could there be a house in that skinny box? Did they send the wrong item?

I dragged the box to the backyard and opened it.

Oh, my goodness! Look at all the parts!

There was a zillion kinds of screws, bolts, and miscellaneous hardware to go with those sides, roof, floor, and door. There was a lot of part A to part B with screw C stuff in the directions. The project might have been a tad more difficult than I had envisioned.

When Bruce and I were sitting on the grass, sorting hardware and laying out side A, side B, side C, etc., he kept sighing, deeply. I think he was visualizing the Yankee game being played on TV instead of envisioning our awesome finished doghouse. But, he didn't complain, just ground his teeth and frowned a lot. He didn't even get mad when, while he was wasting time reading directions, I put side B to side C with the wrong bolts and he had to take it apart. He's a very unflappable man. Probably a good thing or our marriage wouldn't have lasted forty years. He did make some snide comment about not renewing my option last month. I think it was after I ordered several bookcases that had to be put together and there was that mess with the glue on the carpet because I read the directions incorrectly. At least I read the directions that time. I am improving. He still grinds his teeth and frowns—a lot.

The doghouse had a swinging door. We painted Brandie's new house red and white to match our house, added a water bucket to the kennel, and stood back.

Our Siberian Husky's new home was ready. We went after Brandie, put on her spiffy new choke chain and leash, and climbed into the car. She loved riding and gave us happy kisses over the headrests. When we got out of the car and Brandie lunged down the street, I used some of my honed training techniques on her. First lesson for Kathy. Getting an enthusiastic Siberian under control is a bit more complicated than getting a Westie under control. I sustained whiplash and almost threw my shoulder out, but finally, had Brandie heeling up and down in front of our house.

A footnote here. A year later, I actually had a neighbor thank me for the entertainment I provided on a daily basis. I wasn't sure if I should laugh, take the comment as a compliment, or hang my head in shame.

After our first lesson was over, I took Brandie to her new kennel home. She seemed impressed and happy with it as she meandered around, sniffing and checking out every corner. Frosty didn't much like his new friend and companion. He wasn't afraid of her in any way. He barked. Incessantly. As she roamed her kennel, he barked from outside the chain link and seemed really annoyed that she was in his yard. He lifted his little leg every few feet around her new kennel to make sure she understood this was his territory. Brandie liked Frosty. She tried to get close and his spray turned her nose yellow. Yuck! How disgusting! I washed her face and that became an almost daily procedure. Apparently, Frosty was trying to mark Brandie as his own. Or...maybe let her know what he thought of her?

Brandie finally settled down, curled up, and seemed content. All was fine until about 3:00 in the morning. It had started to rain and I was awakened by the most awful howling. It was a cross between a banshee and an elephant in labor. I peeked out of our bedroom window that was just behind the kennel. There was Brandie, sitting in the rain, howling her little heart out. The sound was so mournful, my heart just broke. She looked miserable and sad. Poor baby. Poor honey.

One moment here. Why is she sitting in the rain when she has that beautiful doghouse? Oh, I know! Brandie was used to sleeping in Don's house with her family. She doesn't know what a doghouse is for. I better go help her. I can't have one of my precious pets sitting in the rain. That's cruel and unkind!

It was a warm spring evening, so I went out wearing just my nightie. The rain wasn't coming down hard. I went into the kennel. Brandie was thrilled to see me. She jumped up and gave me a welcoming kiss. Now my pink nightie had wet paw prints on it. I sighed disgustedly, then commiserated with Brandie and explained that she was okay. She just needed to sleep in the doghouse where it was warm and dry. I knelt down, showed her that the door would swing open, and encouraged her to go in, which she did.

Ah-hah! There's that dog trainer streak showing again! I was glowing with accomplishment as Brandie peeked around the door, came out, and gave me a huge, wet kiss. Knocking me down was not her fault. I wasn't paying attention. Now I had a wet fanny, but Brandie was happy. I showed her how to go back in. She did. I stood up. She came out again. I gave her a few loving pats and left.

I dried myself off, crawled back into bed, dozed, and...there's the howling again! This time more pitiful than before. I gave her ten minutes. She howled the entire time. I sighed sadly. I was still feeling sorry for Brandie. After all, she might be homesick or something. Poor furry homesick critter. Poor baby.

I trudged back to the kennel, went in, got pawprints again, and gave Brandie lots of love and pats. (Any dog trainer worth their salt will tell you that I was actually training Brandie to do the opposite of what I wanted. All those pats were telling her, you're a good girl! Howl some more and I'll come out and reward you with a hug. It's called reinforcement. Because I was not a dog trainer worth my salt, it took me several years to figure this out.)

Brandie went in the doghouse, and I went back to bed. Ten minutes later, the howling was mournful. I was feeling less loving and sympathetic at this point. Bruce was snoring. Apparently, the howling wasn't upsetting him like it was upsetting me.

This time, I marched out to the kennel. It was raining harder, and my nightie was plastered to my body by the time I got through the routine of greeting, wet kiss, pawprints, and doghouse. I watched Brandie and then had a brilliant thought. I decided that she really didn't understand that she would be better off in the doghouse. It was a big doghouse. I could easily fit. Maybe I could show her how nice it would be to hang out in it. So, I did what any dog lover would do. I got down on my hands and knees, crawled into the doghouse, and called Brandie.

Wow! What a response! She came charging into the doghouse. Did I mention it had a swinging door? Do you know how a swinging door works? I'll tell you. It swings. Back and forth, back and forth. And, if you're on the inside of a doghouse and the dog comes charging in? My nose healed in a few days.

Brandie was thrilled. She cuddled up next to me. Did I mention it was raining? Do you know how a wet dog smells? I'll tell you. They smell yucky! But then, I was already wet, so what's a little dog hair, slobber, and vile smell added into the mix. So, there we sat. Girlfriends. Safe out of the elements. I talked to her. Brandie was happy. She dozed. So did I. All was good until I got the cramp in my foot. Getting out of that doghouse and stomping on my foot proved to be a trifle difficult with Brandie sleeping in front of the swinging door, but I managed it.

I was in the kennel, hopping up and down, nightie plastered to my shivering body when I had a revelation. What in blazes was I doing out in a rainstorm, sleeping in a doghouse! I gave Brandie a pat and went back in to my house. At least I could stand up there. I changed my clothes. I dried my hair. I curled up in bed. I dozed.

The sorrowful sound filled the air. Blast that stupid dog! I am not going out there again! She can just sit in the rain and howl her dumb head off!

The alarm started buzzing. Bruce yawned, stretched, and drawled, "Why's Brandie howling? Shouldn't you do something about that?"

I bit back the nasty retort, smiled, and said, "She'll be fine. She's just homesick."

The howling went on for several nights. It had nothing to do with the rain. It turned out Brandie loved sitting in the rain. She also loved sitting in the snow, sitting in the mud, and sitting out in ice storms, but those are other stories. She also loved to howl. I decided she was trying to contact other Siberians for a pack meeting of some sort. Or, could it be, she wanted to join my pack in the house?

I was worried about my neighbors. Brandie would howl off and on all night and sleep during the day. I had to figure out a solution. Her sleeping in the house was not going to happen. Our tiny house just barely accommodated Frosty and all of us. So, I came up with a plan. Her kennel was up against our house and our bedroom window. I unrolled the garden hose, took off the window screen, opened the window just enough to slide the hose inside, and turned on the water. Luckily, the nozzle didn't leak so I could leave the outside water faucet turned on.

That night, when Brandie started her howling, I reached for the hose, opened the window, and sprayed her from my warm bed. She jumped up, thoroughly startled, shook off the water, then studied the backyard. She also—shut up.

So much for loving human patience. However, my solution worked! Brandie never did figure out where the blasts of water were coming from, so she didn't blame me. She just started to equate howling with a spray of water. She stopped howling. I felt so proud that I had outwitted her and had absolutely no remorse for the method. I had won round one in the battle of wits. Or did I?

I must admit, visitors to the house would stare at the hose hanging on the inside of our bedroom window. It didn't do much for the decor, but everything did match. I had purchased a green hose to coordinate with my drapes and bedspread.

Brandie adjusted to her new digs. She rarely used the doghouse, but that was her choice.

I spent the summer training Brandie and Frosty. I didn't mind being the source of amusement for Mr. Dog Trainer, his wife, and the class. If I wasn't chasing Frosty, I was chasing Brandie. Both dogs loved the classes and attention. I had control of them and felt in charge. Well, okay, I had control of them most of the time. Some of the time. Often. Sometimes. Okay, I admit it. They might have had control of me, but we were having fun!

About this time, Mr. Dog Trainer mentioned to me that he thought Brandie was an excellent specimen of the breed, and if I was still interested in conformation showing, he thought she might do some winning. However, we were training her for obedience, and dogs shown in conformation had to learn a different set of commands. For example, in obedience they're trained to automatically sit when you stop walking. In conformation, they are trained to stand when you stop.

Do you see the tiny flaw in this scenario? It had taken me months to get Brandie, who wanted to run until she dropped, to even consider sitting when we stopped walking. Now, this man wanted her to stand when I stopped? It boggled my mind. But, I must admit I was intrigued by the suggestion. Mr. Trainer told me about conformation classes that the local kennel club held once a week. He said all you had to do was show up, pay your dollar, and they would teach you how to show in conformation. It sounded like fun to me. I was about to make "dog mistake" number three.

It turned out the kennel club trained at a local facility that was about a mile from our house. I knew Brandie's fatigue level. She didn't have one. I also knew when Brandie's enthusiasm faded. It didn't. So, put this together with taking her into a strange building filled with people I didn't know, who were doing things I didn't understand, and I decided I needed a plan. If I wasn't going to look like an idiot, I had to have complete control of Brandie in this situation. Remember Frosty and the "fun" match?

I came up with a brilliant solution. Instead of driving to the class, Brandie and I would jog on over. That way, Brandie would be tired by the time we got there, and I would have better control. Better yet, I would work her for an hour before we left, and she would have a recent obedience refresher lesson. That combination should give me an advantage.

The night of the class, we walked up and down the sidewalk practicing our obedience lessons for over an hour. Then, we jogged the mile to the class. I don't know if Brandie was tired, but I sure was.

I went up to the door and stood there. There was no glass in it. I hate opening doors when I can't see on the other side. I have this theory that, in a previous life, I probably walked confidently into a room this way and someone set me on fire or something. So, I have a terrible fear of walking into rooms I can't see into. In my cowardly opinion, I think all doors should have a glass window in them.

As I stood there uncertainly, a lady with a poodle came up, smiled, and walked in. I didn't hear any screams of agony, so I gathered my courage and followed her. After all, if someone had a flame thrower, she would be the first to go. Brandie lunged at the poodle. I gave her an authoritative jerk on the collar and stood watching people who had complete control of their dogs with leashes that looked like thin threads. I was totally impressed. So was Brandie.

She was panting enthusiastically, drooling, and trying to figure out a way to get loose and join everyone.

Just then a man and woman came up to me and introduced themselves. Their names were Mae and Pete. They had a beautiful red Siberian Husky with them. He had manners and just oozed success. Brandie was hopping, trying to get near him. I'm sure no one believed I worked with that blasted dog every other day. It was like her manners had simply checked out. She just wanted to romp with her new Siberian friend.

Pete calmly petted her, said he thought she could successfully compete in the conformation ring, and added, "Why don't you run her a couple of miles before you come to class? She probably needs some exercise."

I bit back the nasty retort. After all, I didn't want to alienate my new Siberian Husky friends. I felt like "one of the group," although Brandie's gray, white, and apricot certain didn't compare with their male's deep red coat and almost sparkling white.

They told me about the local Siberian Husky Club. It had been formed the year before and was looking for members. I was thrilled. Imagine that. Other people who loved this breed. Pete explained it was a good way to learn about Siberians, meet people with the same interests, and get training tips. Obviously, he thought I needed those training tips. And, in retrospect, I guess I did.

I watched Mae confidently put the red male through his paces in the conformation class and thought, I can do that. So can Brandie. It doesn't look hard.

There's the old "things that look simple are often not" adage coming through again.

The next week, I enrolled in the conformation class and Brandie challenged my stick-to-it-tive-ness. Week after week, I worked with Brandie, determined to teach her to be a show dog. I was warned by Mr. Dog Trainer that it could be difficult to train a dog in obedience and conformation at the same time because you are teaching opposite responses, but he said it could be done, so I was undaunted.There were other people who had done it.They claimed dogs were intelligent enough to know the difference between the conformation ring and obedience ring. My life philosophy has always been, if someone else had done it, so can I. If they haven't, I still can if I work hard enough. Why, oh why, did God not give me more common sense and less philosophy!

Life was exciting and fun. I was going to two obedience classes on Wednesday evenings and a conformation class on Thursdays. Mr. Dog Trainer had two classes, one following another. I had Brandie in the first class and followed it with Frosty.Thinking back, someone should have given me an award for hutzpah. Or, maybe stubbornness. Or, maybe stupidity. First, I would be embarrassed by Brandie's antics, then by Frosty's. Frosty was smart and knew the routines. Most of the time he did them perfectly. But, sometimes his Terrier instincts would take over and the chase was on. Or, he would get in a snit and pout while he lagged through every exercise.

On the flip side, I had Brandie. I came to realize that Siberians have basic instincts too. Frosty's were to chase, bark, wag, and be happy. Brandie's were to chase, wag, and be happy. I decided Frosty was smarter than Brandie because he had one more attribute than Brandie. It was the "bark" thing. Brandie never barked. I guess it took too much energy, and she didn't want to waste energy for barking that she could use on running. If I had known anything at all about Siberian Huskies, I would have realized that any breed bred to pull a sled and run was going to RUN and PULL whenever they got the chance.

Working Brandie in obedience was borderline lunacy. I never gave up because I loved the challenge and occasional victory. I did, however, get confused occasionally. Like the night I was working Brandie, squinted in concentration, and blinked. Now, I admit that doesn't sound too unnerving. However, I was wearing hard contact lenses.

This was at a time when they hadn't been around too long and still had a few imperfections. One was that they would "pop" out very easily. I felt the lens on my lashes, plucked it off, and kept walking as the class was practicing heeling. Mr. Dog Trainer did not like his class interrupted, but I gathered my courage, broke ranks, and asked him to hold Brandie while I went to the ladies' room to put my contact lens back in.

He seemed offended that I, a mere trainee, would ask the leader to hold a dog. I fled before he could object, hurriedly reinserted the lens, scurried back to the class, then rescued Brandie from Mr. Trainer.

I took a few steps forward and the room spun. I couldn't seem to focus and felt like I was going to fall on my nose. In my panic, I simply handed the leash to Mr. Dog Trainer and fled for the ladies' room. I ignored the "what is your problem, lady!" look on his face.

In the ladies' room, I quickly diagnosed the problem. I had put the lens in the eye that already had a lens. So, I had terrific vision in one eye and practically none in the other. Did you know that if you put two lenses in one eye, your vision is distorted? I mean—really distorted!

I returned to class. As I approached Mr. Trainer, I tried a lame smile and told him what I had done. Much to my surprise, he started to laugh, then gave me the leash, gestured me back into class ranks, and quipped, "Why doesn't that surprise me?"

Apparently, I was making an impression. I'm not sure that it was a favorable one.

Then there was the night when I was heeling with Frosty, and he lunged away. I gave the correction, which was a short jerk on the leash. However, I had worked with Brandie in the previous class and apparently my zoned out mind was in that class. I jerked Frosty so hard he tumbled end over end. Mr. Trainer and the class were aghast, and I got lectured on how I could have broken the poor Westie's neck or trachea. It seemed I had mixed up which dog I had on the end of the lead. I felt guilty for weeks. For years. Oh, I'll admit it. I still feel guilty.

After the "almost broke his neck" incident, I was driving home. Brandie and Frosty were in the back seat. As I drove the miles on a country road, I was so depressed about my inadvertent blunder and my lack of dog training skills, tears started to dribble. I was thinking about giving up the dog game. After all, I was obviously incompetent. Months of training and my dogs were still not the stars of any class. For that matter, they were at the bottom of their respective classes no matter how much time or effort I put into training them.

I was weeping and feeling sorry for myself. Brandie leaned forward from the back seat and plopped her front paw against my neck. Then, she leaned over and licked my tears away. It was as though she was apologizing and feeling sorry for me. In that moment, I felt so much love for those blasted doggie delinquents that I just knew I'd be training them for eternity.

I found myself wanting to learn more about the breeds. But, in those days there wasn't the Internet from which to garner information. Our local library only had a few books on dogs and none that gave me information that I needed on West Highland White Terriers and Siberian Huskies.

I decided to attend dog shows, even if I didn't enter, because there were knowledgeable people and information at those events. Even though I was attending obedience and conformation classes, my breeds weren't in attendance, except for Mae and her gorgeous red male. I had learned a great deal from the Siberian Husky Club I now belonged to, but had an insatiable desire to learn more. I wanted more facts. So, I began to plan for my first American Kennel Club (AKC) all-breed dog show.

After much thought, I decided to keep training Frosty in obedience for fun and switch Brandie exclusively to conformation. I was assured by my Siberian friends that Brandie was a good specimen. I had compared her to the breed standard and she seemed to fit the criteria. She was also getting fairly competent at showing in conformation. I decided Brandie would make her debut at the La Crosse, Wisconsin, all-breed AKC show, the following summer. I began planning, increased our training, and visualized our success.

In the meantime, Brandie was teaching us many things:

1. The wisdom of shortening a leash when another dog approached.

2. The fun of playing in a water bucket, splashing most of the water out and, if your feet are dirty, digging in said bucket, thus cooling your body and turning the water muddy brown.

3. The art of teasing a Westie even though chain link separates you.

4. The skill involved in digging a hole in the yard even though you're on a leash. You get Kathy talking to the neighbor (not hard, Kathy was always babbling about something), and while they enjoy the moment, you dig.

5. The craft of properly moving in and out of a kennel. The technique I devised was—open door a crack, insert hand and arm to push dog back, slide left hip through crack to keep dog in kennel, and slam door quickly to keep dog from escaping.

Even though Bruce and I were especially careful in the—moving in and out of kennel—procedure, Brandie still managed to occasionally escape. This was always an exciting moment or two or ten. Remember the flaw I mentioned when I rambled about "never escaping?" Here it is!

We had almost mastered the technique of keeping Frosty from escaping. It went like this. I opened the house door, turned, and commanded, "Frosty, stay!"

Frosty stood like a rock. I moved through the doorway, and he zoomed past. Did he not know what STAY means? That's what the varmint wanted me to believe. But, I knew better! After all, I had spent big bucks and hours of time teaching him! He knew the word! However, I learned to use my foot, brace it against his little head, and slam the door after quickly pulling my foot out.

He'd look me right in the eye, stand perfectly still, and as I moved out the door, his little body would wiggle happily. If I forgot the foot thing or was dumb enough to trust him, he had perfected the craft of turning into a slithering snake and whipping past me. I'd scream, "Frosty, come!" He'd turn his cute little head, smile, and zoom across the street. Blast that furry little monster!

One chilly autumn morning, I was using my foolproof kennel entrance technique on my way to clean Brandie's estate, when she slipped past me. Now, I will admit to you I may have been daydreaming about an upcoming episode of *Tarzan*, but she really didn't have much room. I started screaming, "Brandie, come!"

Hundreds of dollars spent on obedience classes, and the word "come" didn't seem to compute. I saw her bushy tail disappear around the corner of the house.

I was screaming at her to come when Jason, who was then about four, opened the house door to see what was the matter with Mommy. As he expressed his concern with the door open, you guessed it. There was a blur of yapping white streaking past him. Frosty saw Brandie and the chase was on.

It was, actually, quite impressive. Frosty barking and yapping his head off, little legs churning, while he tried to catch the galloping Brandie. I took off after them. I lost the varmints around the neighbor's house and almost panicked. Then, I heard the yelling. I admit I momentarily toyed with slinking back home and pretending I didn't own dogs, but I have this ridiculous "you must take responsibility for your actions" streak. Taking responsibility really can be annoying sometimes, and it also can be embarrassing.

I peeked around the house and there, by the infamous rabbit hutch, was Brandie standing on her back legs trying to catch rabbits through the mesh wire. Frosty was at her feet yapping and jumping, and the frantic rabbit owner, who thought Brandie was an escaped wolf, was screaming. Panicked bunnies were hopping in all directions. I guess they thought they were about to become lunch. They may have been right.

I raced over, picked up Frosty, who kept right on yapping, and grabbed Brandie's ruff. (We didn't keep a collar on her when she was in the kennel for fear it might snag on something, and she'd hang herself. In that moment, I remember thinking that, next time, I would leave the collar on, and if she strangled herself, it would save me the trouble of doing exactly that.)

I apologized profusely to the neighbor, smiled lamely, and made some inane remark about how I hoped she knew rabbit artificial respiration because I thought her bunny with the spots was having a coronary. I was joking. She didn't think it was funny. Some people have no sense of humor.

Bruce thought the incident was very, very funny. He teased me about getting old and slow. You would think a grown man would know better than to tempt fate that way. A few nights later, Bruce went to feed Brandie. The evening was warm and all the windows were open. I heard him call, "Brandie, come!"

I frowned and thought, Huh? Why's he calling her? She's in the kennel. I...oh no!

I went running outside in time to see Brandie disappear into the neighbor's yard. Bruce was standing there looking thoroughly annoyed. He sighed disgustedly. You would have to personally know Bruce to truly realize the enormity of his deep sigh. He is a quiet man, never yells, is never rattled in any situation, and is the perfect match for my rather passionate responses to situations. I'm an Aries. He's a Scorpio. I had a psychic tell me that was a terrible combination. Hey! It works for us. Most of the time. Some of the time.

Back to Brandie. I told Bruce that he was obviously getting old and slow. He glared at me, ignored the baited statement, and suggested we check out the rabbit hutch.

We ran after Brandie. Sure enough she was tormenting bunnies. This time, the owner didn't know because Brandie's sidekick, the yapping Westie, wasn't there to bust us. As I said before, Brandie did not bark. Most Siberians that I owned didn't either. Howl, yes. Even moan occasionally and talk in a yodel, but they rarely barked.

Bruce reached for Brandie. Her eyes lit up and said, I remember this game! It's called chase Brandie! It was one of Don's favorites. Mine too! Let's go!

She took off, Bruce and I right behind. Brandie teased and toyed with us. She let us catch up and almost get a hand on her, then she'd scamper away. We chased her through yard after yard. Finally, she tired of the chase game and headed home. We had a small patio block area just in front of the kennel. Brandie was sniffing its contents when Bruce made the best defensive lineman tackle I've ever seen. He threw himself at Brandie, wrapped his arms around her, and they hit the ground together. I grabbed Brandie and dragged her back into the kennel. She was wagging happily as I closed the door.

I turned back to Bruce who was standing, grimacing, holding his left hand. He held it out and I paled. I didn't realize fingers could separate at the knuckles and go in different directions. I mean, aren't fingers supposed to be straight and simply bend up and down? Bruce had, apparently with Brandie's help, devised a new way of bending fingers. His was bending from side to side. The base of his finger was straight but, from the knuckle up to the tip, the finger was dislocated. I had never seen a finger dislocated before and was in awe.

I said, "Wow! Look at that! I didn't know fingers could do that!"

He gritted, "So much for wifely sympathy! Help me! Straighten the thing!"

I said, "Excuse me? I'm no doctor. How?" This was my first experience with any kind of major wound. It would not be my last.

He said, "Do it like they do in the movies! Just grab the end and pull! Do something! It hurts!"

"No way! I don't pull anything!"

I took the wincing Bruce to the emergency room and waited in the lobby while a doctor grabbed and pulled! After all, that was his job, not mine. They put this cute little splint on Bruce's finger. It had a nifty blue pad. Bruce was not amused when I told him it made him look macho and I was sure football players had to wear them and had I mentioned how proud I was of his amazing tackle?

The emergency people were very nice. At that time, I didn't know that I would become personally acquainted with most of them. They would in the next seven years learn to recognize Bruce and me on sight, and they enjoyed and were amused by the reasons we were in their care which would vary from unique to down right bizarre and unbelievable.

I took Bruce home, poured him a drink, and commiserated with his pain. Interestingly enough, he never threatened to get rid of Brandie or me. For that matter, he never suggested getting rid of any of the pack of dogs we were about to acquire no matter what havoc they wrought, even though I considered it on more than one occasion.

After the Christmas holidays, I decided we needed another Siberian Husky. Why, you ask? Good question. What happened to all that logic, etc.? Don't know. Gone.

I had been comparing Brandie's conformation to that of other dogs in the Siberian Husky Club and was now aware that she had flaws. My Husky compatriots taught me the value of studying pedigrees and Brandie's was not very impressive. I found myself toying with the idea of breeding. That meant I needed the best foundation stock I could get, and I decided Brandie wasn't it. And, I fantasized about getting a perfect Siberian from a breeder who knew their stuff. I would buy a beautiful Siberian who could easily win.

Plus, think about the advantage of having two Siberians. They could be chums, pull a sled together, and I could have the fun of training a Siberian from puppyhood. The flaws in that statement are so large you could drive a truck through them, but what can I say? I was naïve, enthusiastic, and an idiot!

The "let's add to our pack so we can better compete and have more fun doing it" is a trap dog people fall into. I'll warn all of you out there who have toyed with entering the "sport of dogs" with your one dog. One is seldom enough. It's like eating one potato chip or one cookie. Acquiring can become addictive. It goes like this. If one is great, two will be better, three will be awesome, and four will be.... I'll answer that for you. Four and above is LUNACY, but fun. Does that seem like an odd statement? Could be, but how many lunatics don't know they're lunatics and just have fun being a lunatic? There's a question to ponder.

At this point in time, I simply could not get enough of the Siberian Husky. I loved their antics, their enthusiasm, their tendency to test everything. Perhaps they were very much like Kathy. Hmm. Another point to ponder.

After years of experience with a pack of Siberians, I have decided they are like canine cats. Ever try to train a cat? You don't usually train them. They allow you to enter their space, tolerate your existence, then train you. I know this. Because...you guessed it, I eventually had a few cats. Cats that I adored as much as I loved my dogs.

I fell in love with Siberian Huskies' free spirits. One of the reasons I was not the best Siberian Husky trainer in the world is that I was more inclined to think their antics were funny. I loved the way they challenged everything I tried to do and every situation I put them in. I adored their intelligence and love of all people. That's right. All people. Imagine the blow my ego took when I discovered Brandie loved every person with whom she came in contact. Loyalty was not in her vocabulary.

You do, however, have to let Siberians, and Westies too, for that matter, know you are in charge. You must be leader of the pack. Not superior, merely leader. The enjoyment in having these breeds is to be tough enough to be in charge, appreciative of their intelligence, loving enough so they know you care, and able to laugh at yourself. They laugh with you. They love you. They will follow you. Mine were never...trained. But they were...taught. Also, they had unique senses of humor and knew what was acceptable rebellion and what was not.

I convinced Bruce we needed another Siberian Husky. Friends in the Siberian Husky Club of Greater Milwaukee directed us to a reputable breeder in Chicago.

We met Jorge and Marie, their four children, and their dam (mother dog). There was one show quality, breedable female puppy left for sale. She was black and white and had a wonderful glint in her dark, brown eyes. Marie explained that this puppy had what was called a "coat break." The puppy had a white shoulder that broke into the solid black. At the time, I didn't realize how many judges and breeders felt negatively about this "break." While it was not listed as a serious flaw in the Siberian Husky standard of the breed, it was considered "not desirable."

I hardly noticed the white shoulder. The puppy was beautiful in every way—in body, in temperament, in spirit. She was outgoing, moved perfectly, and had a swagger that I adored. I was a novice, but I loved the way she was put together, her balance and easy way of gaiting, and her attitude. I could see the differences between this puppy and Brandie. I decided the white shoulder was irrelevant.

We bought the puppy, but couldn't take her home because she was too young. We would come back for her in a few weeks. I decided we could trust Jorge and Marie to take good care of our new puppy. My instincts about the puppy, Marie, and Jorge proved to be correct. Marie and Jorge taught us many things about Siberian Huskies, about friendship, about helping each other, and about love of a breed that many other people consider incorrigible. Thirty years later, I still consider them close friends and always will.

We were bursting with excitement and named our new puppy Boettcher's Natasha. Once again, we began making plans. Brandie and the puppy could share the kennel. They would be best pals. It would help ease Brandie's loneliness. Of course, Brandie never indicated she was lonely, but who was noticing?

I mean, how much extra work would one more dog be? This is like the mistaken idea that if you have one child, having one more will be simple because you've done it before and have all the stuff. Ask any mother who has added the second child. The work doesn't double, it...what exactly does it do, Moms? Be honest. Don't give the answer you think everyone wants to hear.

We innocently decided all we needed was another food dish, leash, and collar. I was so excited I could hardly stand it.

One week before we were to pick up our new puppy, I woke up and there was a layer of snow on the ground. I was elated. It was late March and we had SNOW! This was doubly exciting because I had read an article in a local dog sledding club newsletter that proclaimed the joys of a sport called skijoring.

Those who skijored were thrilled with the exhilaration this sport provided. You took your Siberian Husky sled dog type, put a harness on her, attached a rope and handle (looked like the rope used to water ski) to the harness with a leash clip, put skis on your little feet, and your Siberian pulled you across the white tundra. Or, down the sidewalk if you were a city type.

It seemed simple and fun. I had recently given up jumping horses and was feeling a little blue. I needed some excitement. Needed an adrenaline rush. I had already purchased the skijoring kit and a harness.

Of course, I had never skied in my life, but...how hard could it be? You just attached skis to your tiny feet and away you went! When I received the skijoring harness and line in the mail, I had picked up some short skis in a local drugstore. You read right. Drugstore. I had no idea where to get skis and as I was browsing in the drugstore, they had these little short plastic shoe-sized skis for kids. They were about twelve inches long with two plastic straps-one around the ankle and one across the toes.

I have always been good in the "make do" department, so I decided to "make do" and purchased the small plastic skis.

Does anyone notice this may sound like a recipe for disaster? We have one exuberant Siberian Husky. One harness. One skijoring rope. Short red skis. No brakes. And...one idiot. It doesn't take a genius to see where this is heading.

Brandie and I enthusiastically headed for the golf course down the road. We lived on a short street that dead ended against the golf course. We entered the eighteenth fairway. Guess what? Nobody was there. Surprise! I'll bet you thought Wisconsinites golfed in the winter because they're tough. Wrong!

I had the golf course to myself. It was a cold, gray, cloudy day. Notice how I remember the details? We often remember traumas perfectly.

The first thing that gave me pause was that the golf course was on a hill. I had never been on the golf course and didn't know that. But, I decided that was an advantage because Brandie and I could go faster if we were racing downhill. So, with confidence, I harnessed Brandie, attached the rope with a leash clip, took hold of the handle, strapped on my bright red plastic skis, and we stood there. I realized I didn't know how to get Brandie moving. I didn't know about gee, haw, and hike. Most people think mushers use the term "mush" to get their dogs off and running. Not so. The term we were later taught was "hike." Seeing as how I was new at the "mushing" game, I decided "mush" must be the "go" word. So, I authoritatively ordered her to "mush!" Brandie looked at me like...like...what in the blazes are you talking about? Isn't "mush" something you eat? She didn't move a muscle.

Now, does this make any sense to you? The dog that was always bouncing around, straining at the leash, just stood there and looked at me. The telepathic message I was getting was, I can do sit when you stop, I can do stand when you stop, what in blazes does "mush" mean? We're already stopped!

As I was trying to figure out how to get my message across, a lightbulb went on in Brandie's head. She slowly scanned the hill, realized she wasn't being restrained, and suddenly leapt forward and down the hill.

YIPES!

My little feet (okay, big feet) were moving frantically back and forth as we started down the hill. I finally got them quieted, and we were sailing down that hill. Wow! What fun!

The trees lining the fairway were skimming past. The cold air was brushing my face. I felt wonderful and exhilarated!

That is, I felt wonderful until I hit the ground. Just before the bottom of the hill came up to meet us, the ground came up to meet me. I was suddenly laying on my back, looking up at the gray sky and clouds. Now you know why I remember the entire incident so vividly.

I hit the ground so hard, I couldn't move. The pain was excruciating. I laid there thinking I was probably paralyzed for life. I hadn't told anyone where I was going because my kids were in school, and I wasn't dumb enough to tell Bruce of my plans, and I wondered if I would freeze to death before being rescued.

I did, however, hold on to the handle. That, my friends, seems to be a natural instinct for all Siberian Husky owners. They never let go!

Brandie came back and gave me her best noodle. That was a lick, snuggle, and paw. I thought, How nice. I'll be lovingly noodled before I die. At least, it's a pleasant way to go.

After a few minutes, I realized I wasn't paralyzed and managed to sit up. Standing was a great deal harder. Limping home, even harder. During my three-week hospital stay in traction, I decided to hang up my red skis and skijoring rope.

I didn't go directly to the doctor after the accident. You see, we had an appointment to pick up our new puppy, and any crazed doggie person will tell you everything else gets put on hold when there are "doggie" matters to be taken care of.

So, I filled myself full of aspirin, and we brought Natasha home. She was delightful! She was hell on wheels! Or paws! She loved chasing after Frosty. Then, he would turn the tables and chase her around and around our small house, up on furniture, down from furniture, until they both collapsed. I wanted to keep Natasha in the house with us for a while so we could be properly introduced and bonded.

However, it didn't take long for me to realize that Natasha was not destined to be a house dog for as long as I had hoped. But, then, she was supposed to be Brandie's companion in the long term, not Frosty's. We decided it was time for introductions. Natasha's first meeting with Brandie went well. Okay, so we had to untangle some leashes and unwind them from our legs. Exuberance certainly wasn't a problem. Also, it didn't take long to figure out we now needed a fenced back yard. Natasha definitely didn't get enough exercise on the end of a leash or running around our house. I could see all sorts of problems looming in the future. Chasing two Siberians and one Westie to the rabbit hutch was not appealing.

Bruce grumbled and grumbled when I suggested fencing. Handy person stuff was still not his gig. I presented my arguments, and remembering his finger, he decided a fence was probably a good idea. However, we did not know how to put up a fence and didn't know anyone else who did, either. In those days, in Waukesha, very few people fenced their yards. It wasn't necessary. It wasn't often done. People enjoyed the "wide open" feel. However, those people did not have three doggie delinquents to tire out.

So, I went to my source of all things to buy—catalogues. I found woven wire fence at a reasonable price, and the metal fence posts to go with it, in the Sears catalog. It never occurred to me that driving metal fence posts into the ground might be a challenge.

I bought the fence and posts, then hauled them home. When Bruce tried to pound the posts into the ground, guess what? The ground was harder than it looked.

But, I'm getting ahead of my story. Let's back up a tad, to a few days after bringing Natasha home. My back pain grew so intense, I could no longer tolerate it. I went to the doctor. He pressed my lower back and I pitched forward in agony, almost dropping to the floor.

He caught me and said, "You have a back injury."

I thought, No kidding. How surprising. What a revelation. What gave it away? The fact that I came here telling you I hurt my back? The crooked way I walked? My bent over posture? My permanent grimace of agony?

He asked me how I did it. When I told him skijoring, he looked at me like I had two heads or a loose screw. When I told him how you skijored, he closed his eyes and shook his head. It was a look, and gesture, I grew used to seeing on doctors' faces.

My friendly physician put me in the hospital. But, wait a minute. What about the dogs and children? Bruce has to work. This is where Grandma Geri decided she could help out. Now Grandma Geri is a competent person, but had only one child. Bruce. That convinced her she didn't need any more. (When Bruce read that statement, he pouted for a while and wanted me to edit it out. I thought my readers were entitled to that information. This is one of those rare cases where the author wins out over the editor.)

Geri had a dog while Bruce grew up. But, Candy was a well-trained, home-oriented Cocker Spaniel who never got in trouble and never left her own yard. Definitely not in the same class as my hyper Siberians and wound up Westie.

Natasha was still living in the house at this point. Grandma Geri was really upset when she saw Natasha chasing Frosty and grabbing his furry neck. She thought the Siberian was trying to kill him. When I explained by phone, from my hospital bed, that's how Siberians played, Grandma was aghast. She said it was way too rough for Frosty's little body. I asked her did she notice that Frosty often turned the tables, chased Natasha, and bit her ankles to get control? That Frosty was usually the one who started the games? Grandma conveniently overlooked Frosty's antics and decided that Natasha was a murderer in disguise. Her sympathy was with Frosty. I could not convince her that Frosty was tough, enjoyed rough romping and chasing, and often got the upper hand in spite of his size.

Grandma solved her problem by chasing Natasha with a broom every time she went after Frosty. To this day, Grandma Geri will tell you how much she disliked that blasted Siberian Husky. When you mention Natasha's name, Grandma scowls with disapproval and lectures about that nasty Siberian. Frosty comes off as a Westie saint, even though the little beast often started the altercations, then retreated to high ground on the furniture and gloated down at Natasha.

After my hospital stay, I came home to bedlam. Natasha had grown and the romping matches were taking a toll on my well-ordered house. Grandma, blowing a fallen strand of hair off her face, abandoned ship as fast as possible.

It was time for Natasha's move to the backyard kennel. My house couldn't take any more of her boisterous explorations and exuberant wrestling matches. Brandie seemed offended when we plopped Natasha in her kennel home. She didn't like the way the puppy drank from her pail or explored her doghouse. Brandie grumbled. Then, when Natasha decided it was time to romp, she was met with friendliness at first, then teeth. Natasha discovered that Brandie was not the sweetheart and friendly romper that Frosty was.

I learned much later what was really going on. It seems Siberians maintain a "pecking or pack" order. And, in order to do that, they "peck." Because they don't have beaks, they nip, body slam, and smack with their paws. Their romping is really a way to determine who's boss. At first, it will go back and forth from one dog to the other, until one gives up and says uncle in doggie terms. Brandie was not about to roll over and neither was Natasha. Even though Natasha was much smaller, she was determined to be boss. The word "uncle" didn't seem to be in either of their vocabularies.

While Natasha and Brandie romped, growled, threatened, and slammed each other to the ground, Bruce and I turned our attention to the fence. We tried using a hammer to pound the fence posts into the ground. Each metal fence post had an inverted "V" at the bottom to give it stability. Notches ran up the entire length of the post. The notches were where you fastened your wire and then bent down the notches to secure the wire, sort of like a tab. The "V" that gave stability was also a devil to pound in. Especially, with a hammer. You see, they weren't designed for hammer pounding.

We talked to my Dad, and he suggested a sledgehammer, then lent one to us. That was a partial solution. The problem was the posts were seven feet tall, so that when driven into the ground, the finished height would be five feet. Problem? How does a five-foot-eight-inch man, with short arms, bang a seven-foot-tall post into the ground? It was quite amusing to watch. He seemed offended when I laughed.

We solved that problem with a stepladder. Anyone who has installed posts must be on the floor laughing hysterically. There actually was a simple device used to solve this problem. It was called a "post driver." The post driver was a cylinder, with handles, that fit over the post. You pulled it up and let the weighted end of the driver bang the post into the ground as it fell.

Imagine that. A device for driving posts. It took us several years and fencing projects to find this marvelous invention. They didn't carry the post driver in the pages of the Sears catalog. Fencing companies did. Imagine that. A fencing company. Who knew? Not us. What a novel idea. A company that does "fencing things."

For the time being, our stepladder and sledgehammer worked. Not efficiently, but effectively. But, I got really tired of listening to Bruce's whining about his shoulders hurting, and his arms hurting, and his head hurting...and on and on and on. Apparently, sledging and stepladdering weren't in the CPA's job description, and he had no desire to add it.

After the posts, came fastening the wire. Of course, in order to fasten the wire you had to unroll it. Sounds simple, doesn't it? Just unroll the wire. That would be fifty feet of wire that's probably been rolled up for at least six hundred years, which means it's lost its memory of how to "unroll." We had five of these fifty-foot bundles.

We unrolled. It rolled up. Then, Bruce unrolled and I stood on one end. However, when I stepped off, the dumb thing re-rolled. He told me to stay on the end, then tried to fasten his end to the posts. That worked until he got halfway. I had to step off and when I did...zap! Bruce was rolled up in the wire. Not a pretty sight. Bruce was not a happy camper.

Next solution. I unrolled Bruce and the remaining wire, held on, and pulled, while he slowly attached it. It was tough going, but we're tough people. We managed to get the wire inserted under the tabs.

Done yet? Of course not, silly. Naturally, we didn't have the exact amount of wire and were left with several extra feet. Hmmm. I guess the extra should be cut off. How do we do that? We tried tin snips, pliers, an old scissors, then solved our problem by doubling the wire back, fastening it to the post, and leaving it. Not beautiful, but it worked. Oh, by the way, there was also a tool for this job. It was called a "WIRE CUTTER." But, we didn't know that! You may be getting the idea, by now, that Bruce and I were not exactly informed when it came to projects. And, we never had sense enough to ask the right people how to do things. We just tried to figure it out ourselves and blundered ahead.

Are we finished with the fence? I certainly hope so. Uh-oh. There's a wubble in the wire between the posts. How do you pull the wire tight? Years later, we found out there's a marvelous invention for that purpose. It's called...you guessed it...a "wire stretcher." Of course, we didn't have one. We struggled, we pulled, we tugged, we opted for semi-tight.

Next problem. You have to bend the tabs down so they hold the wire in place. Did I mention how thick the tabs were? I should have. Very, very thick. Pliers didn't work. Swearing didn't help. Hammering was tough because when you hammered the tabs, the post started to pull out of the ground and bend toward the neighbor's house. We opted for slightly bent tabs done with pliers. Not correct, but it held.

Several days of working evenings, plus Saturday and Sunday, and our project was complete! We had a semi-tight, slightly wubbled, doubled wire in one corner, fence with posts not driven completely in...yard! Yea! It might not have been perfect, but to us, it looked beautiful. Plus, I had bought green vinyl covered wire so it matched the grass. I always was a woman who had a sense of "fashion." Ask my kids. If it doesn't match, I may get slightly neurotic. That is, if I'm not already neurotic. I'll let you decide that for yourself.

The yard was ready for a test run. We called Sheri and Jason so they could admire the yard. Sheri muttered something about not being able to get to her friend's house through our yard, but I ignored her. We let Frosty out. He tried to run through the fence, bounced off, and looked a trifle dazed. I guess it was that green color blending with the grass. I didn't consider the color would be a problem for the critters to see. Apparently, it was.

Brandie and Natasha were let out to romp and tried mowing the fence down by running through it. But, our wubbles held! And, my girls just ricocheted off. Bruce and I were thrilled. We had outwitted the pack. Not only were our dogs corralled, but the kids as well. We had won a round!

As the dogs romped and played, we could hear the phone ringing. I bolted into the house and answered it. Grandma Geri was upset. Their parakeet, Pretty Boy, had passed through the birdie pearly gates. It seems she found him laying on the bottom of his cage.

Pretty Boy was Bruce's Dad's pride and joy. Dad had spent hours training the parakeet. Pretty Boy took cigarettes from his pocket, sat lovingly on his shoulder, took a bath cupped in his hands under the kitchen faucet, and did numerous cute "bird" type things. Grandma felt responsible for Pretty Boy's demise, even though the bird had succumbed to old age. I commiserated with her, assured her it was simply his "time," and managed to keep from laughing when she told me that she was annoyed with Bruce's Dad, because he chewed her out. It seems Pretty Boy had lain on the floor of his cage for several hours before Grandma figured out that something was wrong. She thought the bird was laying on his back doing a trick. After all, Pretty Boy had quite a repertoire. When she went to Bruce's Dad and congratulated him on training Pretty Boy to lay on his back with his tiny feet in the air, Bruce's Dad was incredulous. Apparently, the backstroke wasn't a trick he had taught Pretty Boy. I soothed Grandma's feelings and assured her Dad's ravings were just an emotional outburst caused by a death in the family.

Chapter Three

Blossoming spring turned into luscious, green summer and I worked hard training all three dogs. Natasha learned fast. Bruce went to conformation class with me, so we could take Brandie and Natasha together. I would proudly work with one, then attend the next class with the other. On Wednesdays, I worked Frosty in obedience. Brandie's first AKC show was two weeks away. I was a nervous wreck as the show quickly approached. (Remember Frosty's debut?) I tried to ignore the sick feeling in my stomach whenever I thought about the looming debut, and kept working on Brandie's manners and conformation skills.

One morning, the next door neighbor came pounding on the door. He was upset and said Brandie and Natasha were fighting. I ran to the kennel. Both girls just looked at me with wagging tails, sparkling eyes, and doggie smiles. I frowned. He said a few minutes ago they were trying to kill each other. I reassured him they were probably playing.

You have to understand the way Siberians play. They bite each other's feet in an attempt to bring their opponent down. No blood or wounds. Just tough romping. They grab each other's ruffs and twist to the side, again trying to bring their opponent to their knees and down. If none of that works, they have no problem grabbing and mouthing whatever part presents itself. They grumble and mutter. But, it's not a fight. It's playtime! Rough playtime. Like football or rugby...Siberian style.

When Siberians are loose and running, they use bumping tactics to upend an opponent. It does look like a fight to those who do not understand. But, let me assure you, I have broken up my share of "fights." There is a major difference and it's actually easy to recognize. It's called blood, damage inflicted, intent to kill or maim, demeanor, and my soaring heart rate. It's terrifying and in no way like "playtime."

At this point in time, I had never seen an actual dog fight, but was confident I knew my girls and their intent. I laughed and told my concerned neighbor they were only playing. He looked unconvinced.

The next day, he was back banging on my door again, claiming a war was going on. I checked the kennel. The girls were happy and wagging. I'm thinking, What is wrong with this man? Doesn't he get it?

I smiled and again reassured him.

This went on for over a week. The man was back almost every day. It seems he and his wife were watching the girls and were appalled that I wouldn't do anything. I was getting slightly annoyed. One day, while making the bed, I glanced out, froze, and studied those delinquents. What the? Sure enough! The girls were trying to kill each other. In a friendly sort of way. But, the snarls and demeanor moved me to action.

By the time I got to the kennel, they were smiling and wagging. I watched them interact and got a cold feeling in the pit of my stomach. There was something in their stance and eyes that was unnerving.

When Bruce came home, I said, "We've got a problem." Those were words he would hear many times in the future, and his reaction was always the same. A slight wince and tightening of his lips. Eventually, he got to the "lips turn white" phase, but that was a year or two away.

I had come up with a way to separate the girls. We would divide the kennel in half with a chain link panel, then get a second dog house and water bucket. That way, when unsupervised, the girls could not get at each other. True, it would reduce the space each dog had, but the original kennel was large. Plus, they were let out several times each day to run in the yard and worked with in some way. The kennel was actually more a place to rest and sleep, so the size didn't have to be huge.

We made the necessary changes, and once again, I had control. I could let the girls out to play and, as long as I was present, there were no altercations. They would bump and romp. Frosty would chase and bark. I reveled in their athleticism.

True, I had to be aware of where they were because part of the game seemed to be "let's knock 'Mom' on her fanny." And, true, if I was inadvertently out in the yard in my fuzzy slippers, Frosty would spend his time viciously attacking my feet. So, there I would be, walking around the yard, clipping weeds from the base of the fence (oh yes, that was a problem we hadn't foreseen and increased our workload), sidestepping wrestling Siberians, and shaking Frosty off my feet. Now, granted, most people don't clip weeds in fuzzy slippers, but you have to understand something about my personality.

I get distracted easily. I start out to do one thing and end up doing something else without knowing why or when I changed course. So a trip to the yard in fuzzy slippers to check on the kids could turn into a "oh, let's let the girls out to romp." And while I'm supervising them, there are some weeds that need clipping. And, Frosty might as well get some exercise and where are the clippers? Oh, in the garage. Let's straighten that shelf where the clippers are. That's right, I was going to clip weeds.

I'd step out of the garage, get decked by charging Siberians, and have to disengage Frosty from my slippers. That is, if he didn't pull one off and run away with his prize. Of course, that meant chasing after him and now I was included in the romping as Natasha and Brandie tried to catch us. I happily joined the game, chasing and laughing at their antics.

During one of our play periods, my back went out again. The pain is excruciating when that happens. And, it was only one week until our dog show. I was inconsolable. I had practiced for months, Brandie was trained, and our entry fee was paid. During my sobbing session, Bruce gamely offered to show Brandie.

I was aghast. He had no conformation class training and had never worked with the dogs. Now, granted he loved them dearly, and they loved him, but his idea of discipline was to chuckle and let them lick his chin. Bruce convinced me that he didn't mind not knowing exactly what to do. He had watched me in class and said it didn't look all that hard. I was more than mildly annoyed by that remark, but let it go. After all, he was trying to help me.

Bruce said it didn't matter if they didn't win or even place. We would still garner something from the experience. He said he'd just do what everyone else did and follow ring etiquette. No problem. Brandie seemed trained to him. It was no big deal.

No big deal! I had been working for months for this day. But, I knew I couldn't show her. I could barely walk, and Brandie was as trained as she was going to get. I reluctantly agreed, hoping Bruce wouldn't make too much of a fool out of himself. Because if he did, I would be responsible for putting him in that situation. He just grinned and told me to show him the basics. So I gave him a lesson in the front yard. My heart sank as I watched them. Brandie and Bruce were not exactly a smooth team. But, they seemed to be enjoying themselves as they bounced. She sort of stood still for him when I tried to go through the ritual of examining her.

If I hadn't wanted to see what went on at an official show, I would have cancelled. But...come Saturday morning, we loaded our car with two squabbling kids and Brandie. We headed for La Crosse, Wisconsin, which was a four-hour drive from our house.

You have to understand something about show people. They'll drive anywhere, any distance, during any kind of weather to get to a dog show. Four hours didn't seem like that much. Jason and Sheri were a bit crowded in our small car with Brandie in their laps. But, I ignored the whining, complaining, and arguing. After all, we were on a mission!

We drove onto the show grounds. It was awesome. Dogs of every description meandered around. There were tents, rings, vendors, and people grooming. I fell in love with the atmosphere. The ring we were to show in was indoors.

We checked Brandie over, bought a catalog, found our names in the book, beamed with pride at seeing Bruce, Kathy, and Brandie listed, went to our ring, and picked up the numbered armband. I was a nervous wreck. What had I done? I was sure Brandie would make a fool out of Bruce. She was excited and not listening very well. I told him I didn't mind if he backed out.

He just smiled and said, "Calm down! We'll just do our thing and it'll be over."

Off they went to stand in line. I took Sheri and Jason, found a seat, and prayed that Bruce and Brandie just made it around the ring without a major problem. I told God I didn't care if they took last place, just please get them out alive.

Bruce was amazing. He just went with the flow. Brandie cooperated, even though, when he bent down to straighten her collar, she gave him a kiss. I was breathing a sigh of relief until the judge pointed to Bruce. I thought, Oh no! He's being kicked out.

No. Not kicked out. He had won. Not only that, he went on to take winner's bitch which gave Brandie one point toward her championship. He beat every experienced handler in the ring.

It was unbelievable. I was stunned. I had worked for months to learn the tricks of the trade, and Bruce won without one lesson. You folks see my dilemma? Was I thrilled because they won or disgusted because Bruce just ambled in and made it look simple?

We had a photo taken that I have to this day. It's a reminder not to take life too seriously. Because, sometimes, just a happy attitude and a bit of confidence is all that's needed to win the day. In the years that followed, I witnessed hundreds of people intensely focusing on the perfect way to show. They forgot the pleasure that can be had by enjoying the moment, the dog, the people, the atmosphere. Winning seemed to be all that mattered.

True, Bruce won, but he was enjoying the experience before that happened. Then, he reveled in the win. He enjoyed Brandie. He enjoyed talking to the people who congratulated him. He enjoyed rubbing my nose in his victory. Whoops! What did I just say? Sorry. That just slipped out.

All the Siberian exhibitors were kind and congratulated us. They invited us to their tailgate party. Several of them had also won and the mood was happy. They were celebrating with Cold Duck. We all reveled in the moment. It was a wonderful beginning to years of dog shows and celebrations.

Autumn came and the weather turned brisk in the evening and warm in daytime. Trees turned those wonderful shades of red, gold, and yellow. This time of year in Wisconsin is more beautiful than I can describe and I always relished it. Your senses are stimulated in every way. Colors are vibrant. The air smells fresh and clean. Beautiful, colored leaves flutter from trees under a light breeze. They scrape across pavements, gather on lawns, and are raked into piles that children delight in jumping into.

I concentrated on the conformation classes with an eye toward our next show and victory, then enrolled

Natasha in obedience. Brandie's enthusiasm seemed almost lethargic in comparison to Natasha's puppy antics. I was spending hours and hours in training classes, working the dogs daily, and grooming my poodle clients. I thrived on the doggie activities.

The Siberian Husky Club was having an outing in the state forest. One of the members was going to demonstrate sledding techniques using a "rig." I had no idea what a rig was, but couldn't wait to find out. Club members brought food, and the outing turned into a doggie picnic. I watched in awe as the rig was brought out. Dog sled drivers use this vehicle to train their dogs when there is no snow. It looked like a Roman chariot without sides. It had three rubber tires—two in back, one in front. The steering wheel looked like a scooter handle. The rig had a small floor and brake pedal.

After we all oohed and aahed over the vehicle, we were shown the gangline (the long line which attaches to the front of a rig or sled). It was explained that, after the dog harnesses are put on the dogs, the animals harnesses are attached to the gangline with clips.

Four trained sled dogs were hooked up and the rig owner started giving Siberian owners a ride down the forest's hiking trails. He explained that you stand up on the rig and have to be careful not to oversteer because that causes tipping. To stop you stepped on the friction brake. The dogs took commands from the driver. The only way to steer them was to shout, loudly!

I was a trifle dubious about my riding as I watched the rig careen up and down the trail. There was something about riding standing up that sent chills down my spine. Perhaps it was the memory of my last ride standing up on the short, red skis.

I managed to gather my courage and took my first, and last, ride on a rig. I cannot possibly convey the combination of exhilaration and sheer terror I got from riding that rig. In those days, we were told a Siberian Husky running flat out could do about twenty miles per hour in a sprint. I don't know how fast they were going, but it felt like ninety miles per hour as we bumped along the trail.

Riding a rig is definitely not for the faint of heart. And, even though I had jumped horses, I found this vehicle to be extremely intimidating. There was no feeling of having control. At least, when a horse is sailing over a jump, you have the illusion of control. Riding the rig was more like flying just a few feet above the ground, waiting to smack into something. It didn't take much to tip the rig, especially on the turns. Eventually, I mastered dog sledding, but never trained my sled dogs using a rig.

Instead, I used a bicycle. That's right, a bicycle. Looking back, I have to wonder about the logic that told me a bike was safer than a rig. It may have had something to do with using one dog instead of several but, did I not learn anything from my skiing mishap? Apparently not. Did I have any common sense at all?

There are those who would say the bike was far more fragile and dangerous than the rig. That argument may have merit. I would harness a dog, tie him to the handlebars, and go racing down the hiking trails in the state forest near our home. We covered ground at an amazing speed, and it was a terrific way to train a lead dog. The ground was uneven, and occasionally, we skittered to and fro, but I never hit the ground and was never hurt doing this. I loved it!

But, years later, I would try to discourage my teenage daughter from doing the same thing. I think that shows, deep in my heart, I knew this was a dangerous practice. Incidentally, she did it in spite of my warnings. I'm sorry she inherited my "adventurous" genes. I never worried about what might happen to me. I always worried about what might happen to her. She gave up the practice after sailing over the handlebars on a country road and painfully scraping her body.

We had musher friends who actually used a Volkswagen body, with the engine removed, to train their teams. This should give you an idea of how strong Siberian Huskies are.

They're not big dogs. Our males weighed about fifty-five pounds, our females around forty-five. But, pound for pound, they have amazing strength. In later years, Sheri entered one of our males in a weight-pulling contest put on by the Alaskan Malamute club. He pulled seven hundred fifty pounds from a dead stop. We had a friend who routinely entered weight pulls. Her Siberian Husky exceeded that figure many times.

Back to our doggie outing. The enthusiasm of harnessed dogs waiting to run is impossible to describe, but I'll try. Siberians who have had an experience pulling and running cannot get enough of it. They thrive on it. They relish the moments. The minute they see the harness coming, they hop, they bounce, they jump for joy. This provides a challenge for the person doing the harnessing, but you develop a method of holding the dog with one hand and sliding the harness on with the other. You can train them to stand still, but we didn't want to dampen their enthusiasm in any way, so we always put up with their antics.

Next, you fasten them to the gangline. Then, you hold on for dear life while the rest of the team is harnessed and hooked up. Experienced drivers have better control of their teams and do not put up with the nonsense that we amateurs enjoy as part of the game. They teach their dogs to stand and wait until the starter yells.

Once the team was ready, you let go and got out of the way as quickly as possible as they charged down the trail.

I had personal experience with the "get out of the way as quickly as possible." Several years after our first rig experience, we had our very own team of three. Bruce spent one winter season racing in Wisconsin. I was his "support" staff. One frigid race day (it was fifteen degrees below zero), we hooked up his three-dog team and I gamely let them drag me to the starting line. I held on, tightly, as the lead dog fought to run down the trail.The starting guy started the countdown from ten backwards. I held on and, when he hit zero, I let go and tried to run to the side. My boots slipped on the frozen snow. I lost my footing, slipped down, and my loyal Siberians and loving husband just drove over me. Bruce did yell to get out of the way, I was slowing them down as they careened over me. So, at least, he noticed me under the runners.

Lesson? Never get between Siberians, a crazed competitive husband driver, a sled, and a wide-open trail in winter.

Now, you would think the spectators and other mushers standing around would be running to my aid as I lay in the snow. Someone did offer a hand up, but all the laughing did not sound very compassionate.To soothe my feelings, I found the coffee and sipped. While Bruce was out mushing and enjoying the trails, his "support" staff was freezing to death.

We were out in the middle of the Wisconsin woods. It was forbidden to run the car engine, to keep the heater going, because using gas in that manner might mean walking home.There weren't any gas stations anywhere close. I had on a thick snowmobile suit, but was shivering.

Mushers never shiver and have little compassion for their "support" staffs. Sledding is hard work. It's not just about riding. Good mushers pedal and run behind the sleds, when the going gets tough, to save on their dogs.The exertion is tremendous, and those people are incredible athletes. The idea that mushers ride and loaf is a misconception. Dogs and mushers have to be in peak condition. Even in the biting cold, many of the mushers would shed their jackets when competing.

After drinking coffee to try to warm up, I had a problem. One that could only be solved with a restroom.

I asked, "Where is the restroom?"

They pointed. The outhouse was about one hundred feet away. I was aghast! I was horrified! I was a city girl! We didn't do...outhouses! There had to be...no there wasn't.

My friend and I trudged to the wood shack, and she agreed to stand guard. I went in and discovered the disadvantage of a snowmobile suit. For those of you who have never worn one, they are one piece and zip up the front. It was fifteen below zero. That was not with the wind chill factored in. That was the bloody temperature. Guess what? That is really, really cold and exposed skin gets very uncomfortable. I was in a wooden outhouse with a screened window for ventilation. I had to unzip and practically undress to solve my problem. I won't go into the "sitting" on a wood seat and the sensation that invokes. Let's just say you do your business in a hurry!

After that experience, I decided hot coffee might warm me up, momentarily, but wasn't worth the necessity of what followed.

But, on that warm autumn day, the mechanics of dog sledding weren't on our minds. We were fascinated watching those marvelous animals run the way they were bred to do. We were smitten with the harnessing, training tips, and enthusiasm. Bruce and I decided that, while we didn't have a place to use a rig, we could dog sled down the alley behind our yard and on the golf course. We decided Brandie and Natasha would become sled dogs.

Brandie was harnessed, hooked onto the rig, and given a lesson. She loved it! She was fast! She was unbelievable!

We did not hook Natasha up because she was still a bit too young. Dogs shouldn't be used to pull loads until their bodies have matured. But, we could tell, by the glint in her eye, that Natasha would be just as enthusiastic and exuberant as Brandie. We would have a two-dog team!

We went home and made plans. We would buy a dogsled and harnesses and become mushers!

Through our dog friends, we found a man who handmade sleds. Of course, we had never seen a dog sled, but they had been described to us. When Bruce talked to the sled making man, he was told the sled would be bolted, not tied. Experienced mushers, at that time, preferred to have the sled tied with rawhide at the joints as this gave more flexibility in the corners.

We decided the bolted sled would fit our needs, especially as the tied sled was several hundred dollars more in price, and we were novices. We placed our order and impatiently waited.

We found another man who made sled-dog harnesses and equipment. We ordered two harnesses plus a gangline. Just the arrival of the harnesses and gangline got our adrenaline flowing as we pictured ourselves on the sled cruising down the alley. We waited several months, and finally, the call came. Our sled was ready.

The trip to pick it up required a long drive, but we didn't care. The craftsman proudly showed us our new acquisition. Bruce and I glanced at each other. The sled was six feet long from the runners' back tip to the front. Hmm. They don't look that big in pictures.

I knew what Bruce was thinking. How are we going to get this thing home? We were driving a small Ford sedan.

The sled maker also pointed out the claw brake and explained, when you're standing on the runners which jut out behind the sled and you want to stop, you balance on one foot and push the claw brake down into the snow-covered ground. The brake is fastened to the body of the sled and protrudes between the back runners.

Wait one moment! We're dashing down the trail, hanging onto the sled, and we have to balance and do what? My skijoring and rig training experience flashed through my muddled brain and my guardian angel gave me a slap upside the head. The word "idiot" careened around my brain, especially as our new sled maker friend continued to say that the brake didn't work all that well when Siberians are going full throttle. So, we shouldn't count on it to stop the team, depending upon how many dogs are running and how strong they are.

Wait another moment! You have a brake that doesn't brake? Does that make sense to anyone? I have an idea! Let's invent a brake that "brakes!"

The sled maker said that trained dogs know "whoa" and will stop. It's an important command to teach them. Like...duh! I guess so! Did Brandie and Natasha know "whoa?" Nope! Uh-oh. A glitch.

He smiled and said, "Well, the brake might slow them down a tad and break their momentum."

A tad? Break their momentum?

I had personal experience with...a tad...and ended up in traction for three weeks!

Then, he explained about a "snow hook." It's attached to the sled and you hook it where? Slow down! I don't get this stuff! I thought it would be easy. You just ride! Well, apparently not. It seems the "snow hook" was like an anchor. You could wrap it around a tree or "hook" it into the snow to secure your team. Hmm. This seems a bit uncertain to me. And...how secure is secure?

He was going on and on about "gee means right and haw means left." That's stupid. Why not just shout "right!" "Left!" Why the gee and haw stuff? It gets confusing. Right and left I know. Gee and haw mean—one minute. Which is which!

Then, he laughed about people who think you holler "mush!" It's "hike!" Now I have another problem. I don't get "hike." He said the word sounds like the sound dogs make when they're excited and yiking to go. Let's slow this down and do it logically. Why am I shouting "hike?" Why not, "Let's go!" or "Onward" or a million other logical words. And "gee and haw?"

Holy cow, there's a whole other language involved with this! I understand whoa. But, those other words are confusing. I would come to understand "whoa" a whole lot better in the future. Of course, "mush" makes no sense either.

Okay, now we have some fundamentals. We have to learn other words for common ones. We have a six-foot-long vehicle with a useless brake that wild-eyed, enthusiastic dogs are going to be pulling. And in an emergency, we wrap the snow hook around a tree. What if there's no tree? Stick it in the snow and pray.

How about steering?

He laughed and explained you just shift your weight as the dogs careen around the corners. The sled will follow the dogs. Sort of. Stiffly, sort of. The stiffly is because of the bolted sled. Tied ones work better. Now he tells us. I came to realize, in later years, that the difference between bolted and tied is rather like the difference between luxury car and sub-compact. The luxury car glides up and over tough terrain. In a sub-compact you fight the urge to open the door and pedal. Tied sled—you lean and glide around the corners. Bolted sled—you manhandle (or womanhandle) and sweat around the corners.

He continued to explain that you just hop off the runners, manhandle, and manipulate the sled to follow the dogs, and hop back on. Hmmm. We might have another glitch in the making. He's talking about balance, agility, and strength. I wasn't known for any of that stuff. Bruce, on the other hand, was, and by the gleam in his eyes, I knew he was envisioning himself careening down a snow-covered trail. I was envisioning myself splatting into a tree. It gives the term "tree hugger" a whole different meaning.

After another hour discussing the pros and cons of sledding, we were ready to head home with our new purchase. I decided, while the sled maker was doing "man talk" with Bruce, that I could handle all this sledding stuff. At that time, I weighed about 130 pounds. I'm 5′7″ and had a slender build, but I never considered that I might not be physically strong enough to handle that stiff sled and two hyper Siberians intent on running.

I think I'm missing the "common sense" gene of which we spoke on previous pages. My enthusiasm has always overridden any common sense. So, as the guys talked, I was envisioning my first ride through fresh-fallen snow on my new sled. I knew Bruce and the sled guy were excluding me from the equation, but I was an independent, free-spirited woman, especially while Bruce was at work and out of sight. What he could do—I could do—and probably better. Attitude was never something I lacked.

The guys dragged the sled to the car and suddenly the sled maker frowned and said, "Don't you guys have a roof rack or trailer?"

Roof rack? Trailer? What's he talking about? How do you "rack a roof" and what kind of trailer is he talking about? We didn't know anything about either one. Uh-oh. The sled's almost as long as the car.

I quipped, "I suppose it won't fit in the trunk. Ha-ha."

Mr. Sled maker didn't think that my comment was amusing as I chuckled at my joke while envisioning the sled hanging out of the trunk with a red flag attached. Of course, we didn't have a red flag, but the sled wasn't going to fit in the trunk anyway.

After discussing possibilities, the guys decided they could lash the sled directly to the roof for the ride home, and did exactly that. As we bumped along the country road, you could hear the sled ever-so-slightly sliding around. Of course, that's what sleds are supposed to do—slide around. However, the sled had steel affixed to its wood runners to keep the runners from wearing.

Question: Do you know what happens when steel runners grate across a metal car's painted roof? Answer: Your husband's teeth grind, and the muscle in his jaw twitches as he pictures tossing his wife and her "I got an idea" out of the car.

Our guardian angels helped us get home safely. By this time, Bruce's lone angel had recruited a few more. I think there might have been an angel conference and some suggestions that Bruce's association with me was definitely going to put him in jeopardy. It seems the angels and guardians thought they had picked an easy human—a CPA—accountant type to oversee. Little did they know that he would blunder and select Kathy the daredevil as a mate. I think my team of twenty-five guardian angels started giving advice to Bruce's growing team.

And, give me a break, it didn't cost all that much to repaint the scratched car roof. And, no, we didn't have a blanket or something to put between the roof and the sled. Had that idea occurred, which it didn't, we wouldn't have had one with us anyway.

Okay, now we bought the sled, the harnesses, and the gangline. We have two Siberians, a newly-fenced yard, a kennel run, a doghouse that matched our house, plus an assortment of dishes, brushes, leashes, etc. How much can a roof rack cost? Instead of planning and saving for elaborate vacations, we were investing in—what exactly were we investing in? I know! Adventure!

Hmmm. It seems that our free Siberian Husky wasn't so "free" after all.

We impatiently waited for a snowstorm. It seemed like we always had snow on the ground until we wanted SNOW ON THE GROUND! Suddenly, snow had stopped falling. We watched weather reports. Weeks went by without snow. Finally, we got a dusting overnight. For you folks that don't live in "snow country," a dusting is just what it sounds like. It's a fine layer of snow that just barely coats surfaces and can swirl away under a strong wind. Any musher worth his salt knows that a dog sled will not slide across a dusting. The runners slice through "dusting." I know this for a fact. We tried to push the sled across the dusting and it just grated to a halt. We put the sled away and impatiently prayed for snow.

Finally, we got a couple of inches of the white stuff that could support the sled. This is still not great sledding, but we decided we could make do. We dragged the sled to the alley entrance. We harnessed our dogs. Bruce got on and yelled, "Hike!" Brandie leapt forward. Natasha leaned into the harness, met resistance, blinked a few times, turned around, and glared at us. The message was quite easy to understand. It went something like this. "Hello! I am a show dog. You expect me to pull this thing? Are you out of your mind? I don't do...work!"

Apparently, that gleam I saw in her eye at the rig outing wasn't about leaning into a harness and working. Instead, it was reflecting the thought that Brandie was an idiot for working with the peons!

Brandie was straining to pull. Natasha just sighed as though Brandie was out of her mind. I decided to help Natasha and show her what to do. I grabbed her harness, pulled, and helped. The sled jerked forward. Natasha looked offended, both by the sled and me, but we were dog sledding down the alley!

Does anyone notice a flaw in this scenario? Well, let me point it out. Why was *I* pulling the sled? I had two sled dogs that were supposed to be doing the work! It seems that Bruce had a three-dog team—Kathy, Brandie, and Natasha. And, I wasn't even the lead dog! Merely a worker!

Brandie was in her glory. Her enthusiasm was palpable. Natasha seemed happy to be running alongside of me. It must have reminded her of the obedience and show rings. At any rate, after several runs up and down the alley, Natasha decided to help out and put her back into it. Sort of. She was smart enough to keep the line tight, but I never did see a muscle bulge, even though she was part of our sled team for a short time. We have a wonderful picture of Bruce sledding across the golf course with Brandie and Natasha pulling the sled. But, I always suspected that Brandie did most of the work and Natasha went along for the "run of it."

We were hooked! Bruce and I loved it! Even though we had to do our share of pushing, pedaling, dragging, and running, those minutes of actually riding were worth the work. What a rush!

That winter, we spent every possible moment sledding up and down the alley and took a few rides across the golf course. Now, granted, it wasn't much of a ride, but, as our confidence grew, we started looking for other worlds and trails to conquer.

Spring came, lawns turned green, and trees blossomed. We reluctantly put away our sled and focussed on showing once again. Brandie took another point and, while we were having a picture taken with the judge, that incorrigible Siberian had a snack. The judge had knelt down next to Brandie and me to make the picture more "intimate." As I chatted with the judge, Brandie helped herself to the corsage pinned to the judge's dress, gently nibbling on its petals. My eyebrows shot up and I disentangled Brandie from the flowers as I apologized profusely. Petals framed her Siberian grin. Lucky for me, the judge had a fabulous sense of humor and laughed. She continued judging with half a corsage. It took an hour for the blush to fade from my face. Up to that moment, my confidence had grown. I had taken a point! I had control! Well, I still had taken the point, but control? Maybe not.

About this time, we decided to buy Frosty a dog crate to put him in when we were gone. I had listened to many arguments for "crating." My first reaction was, how cruel to put a dog in a cage. But, most of my Siberian friends used them. Mr. Dog Trainer recommended them, saying dogs felt secure in a proper sized crate, not confined. Plus the crate gave owners a measure of control. I was dubious, but went ahead with the purchase. At that time, Frosty was being left in the kitchen at night.

I put the crate in our bedroom so I could reassure him if the crate was upsetting. But, Frosty took to it like a duck to water. He seemed pleased to have his own den. I was shocked by his response. Of course, this meant he slept in our room at night. I think he enjoyed sharing the bedroom with his human pack.

Frosty even got so all I had to say was, "Get in your crate," and he joyfully obliged. Occasionally, during the day, we would find him snoozing in it with the door open. Our Westie preferred the crate to the isolation of the kitchen. Apparently, he decided it was his own personal den, and he often chose to use it on his own.

We began using the crate in the backseat of the car when only Frosty was a passenger. I could see that, in case of an accident, he was much safer confined than loose.

We had many dogs through the years and, from that day forward, we crated them. Some obeyed like Frosty and seemed eager to "den up," some objected with howls of displeasure, some ran away and had to be captured, but in the end, they all accepted their "dens" as part of a normal routine. By using this tool, I never had to worry about damage to our home when we were gone. I had a place to put dogs when we had guests who didn't like or feared them. And, the crate kept the dogs safely confined when we drove.

I never had a dog's psyche ruined by the experience of being crated.

I grew to view dog shows much like college courses. I learned about nutrition and how to interpret the importance of ingredients listed on dog food bags. I used the best dog food we could afford, and our dog's health reflected that. I learned about assessing a dog's movement to detect anatomical flaws. I came to understand proper dog structure and why it is necessary for optimum efficiency. I watched thousands of hours of judging, not only of my breeds, but every other one, and in the process, came to see what judges look for. I critiqued dog temperament, talked with breeders, and listened to their views, experiences, and goals. I learned about interpreting pedigrees and the importance of bloodlines. I learned what dogs need in order to be happy, healthy, and well adjusted. I simply could not get enough information and looked forward to each show with anticipation.

And, as I watched hours of obedience competitions, I came to a conclusion about training. I decided that it's important to understand the way your particular breed thinks and instinctively responds, then use that information in teaching. And, I pondered this: do you breed to suit the needs of the trainer and pet owner, thereby making training easier? Or, do you breed to keep the Siberian Husky's, or West Highland White Terrier's, or any other breed's original working traits? Of course, all breeds must learn to listen and obey. All breeds must know who is in charge and it cannot be the animal—the canine animal, that is.

We went to Siberian Husky Club meetings, learned from fellow enthusiasts, and shared our sledding experiences. We were told that two dogs just weren't enough if you wanted a real thrill ride. A seed had been planted, one that began germinating almost immediately.

About that time, one of the dog club members had a proposition for me. Mae had a three-month old male show dog that she was interested in co-owning. The deal was, I would get the dog for free, but be responsible for his expenses, for training, and for showing him. She would have a say in any stud dog arrangements. Mae was very particular about breeding. She explained about x-raying both males and females for hip displaysia, carefully critiquing breeding stock's strengths and flaws, checking for eye problems, and assessing pedigrees for genetic faults. Mae taught me about the ethics of breeding. Responsible breeders care about the breed, their individual dogs, dogs that are produced, and where the puppies go. They also enjoy educating the public about the kind of dog they breed.

Up to that time, I had only toyed with breeding my girls. It was a responsibility I wasn't sure I wanted. But, the idea of having another show dog and sled dog to add to our team excited me.

Bruce and I discussed taking on another puppy. In retrospect, we didn't realize the impact of adding a male to our pack. We decided to visit and look at the dog. Big mistake! He was gorgeous, loveable, full of life, and oozed potential. I had to have him. Bruce wasn't so sure, but I pleaded, and he gave in.

We signed the papers and took the puppy home. I named him Baku. Bruce and I decided we needed a kennel name to put on our show dogs and came up with BRUKA—a combination of the first three letters of Bruce's name and the first two of mine. We loved the name. Mae's kennel name was Amorak, so Baku became Amorak's Baku of Bruka. It sounded so wonderfully official. Baku was outgoing, friendly, and had the perfect temperament for the show ring. Later, he and Sheri won many, many Junior Showmanship competitions together. He was a beautiful Siberian Husky—richly black and white and perfectly marked. He had a lovely head, well-set ears, balanced gait, big dark brown eyes, and was extremely intelligent.

He loved to romp, as all puppies do, but was more subdued than Natasha had been. We just knew he would fit in perfectly. But, I guess it's like having your mom select a blind date for you. Your mother's tastes in the opposite sex are rarely yours.

Our girls would not allow the gorgeous Baku to be kenneled with them. They made his life miserable and took "picking on and pecking" to a new level. Apparently, the girls were trying to make Baku understand that this pack was led by females and he was lowest on the totem pole. That meant Baku had to be kept in our tiny house, which seemed tinier with him zooming around.

This should have been a possibility I considered before we brought him home. But, my specialty is hindsight, not foresight. I have apologized for that flaw so many times, the speech is memorized and quite boring.

Our small house had only two bedrooms. Jason and Sheri shared one and, as they were getting older, they really needed their own rooms. Added to that, we discovered the city in which we lived only allowed two dogs per household, so we had an additional problem, one that many people who get into dog showing run into—dog licensing limits in many cities, towns, and villages.

I had always harbored a dream to live in the country and often drove out of the city along winding country roads to admire farmlands, barns, animals, trees, and forests.

We made the decision that we needed a larger house for the family and a big yard for the children and dogs. In order to legally keep our dogs, it had to be in the country where they allowed larger numbers to be kept and licensed.

We started looking for a house to buy.

Do you see how this thing was mushrooming? I was a normal city girl slowly being converted to...hmmm. Converted to what? That's a good question. Converted to something, that's for sure. The amazing thing is...I didn't even know it was happening.

Chapter Four

After a dedicated search, we found the perfect home in the country. Well, okay, maybe it wasn't perfect, but it had potential. You know the term "fixer upper?" My advice to you is, fully investigate that term when it's applied to something you want to purchase and live in. It seems no one else would buy the home because it was an unconventional concrete pre-formed panel house. However, we were undaunted. That could be because we were naïve and didn't do our homework. But, the house and property had other requirements that fit our needs. The home was three bedrooms on five acres in the country, and we could legally have up to eight outside and two inside dogs.

Notice the lack of concern about property value increasing over the years, resale potential, etc? All I thought about was space and not having neighbors too close.

The house was an experimental design in those days. Twelve-foot high by four-foot wide panels of concrete were pre-poured in a factory. They were made up of two inches of concrete, one inch of insulation, and two more inches of concrete. The panels were brought to the site, configured in the desired floor plan, and buried four feet into the ground for stability. The roof was conventional and the builder assured us the structure would stand up in a tornado as it had a bunker-like quality. The roof might go off, and the windows blow out, but the structure would stand. This was important because an occasional tornado did rip through the East Troy, Wisconsin area. Also, on rare occasions, straight-line winds can reach 75–100 miles per hour and do tremendous damage.

Our new house did not have a basement. It was built on a concrete slab. This was highly unusual in our area, as basements housed washers, driers, water heaters, and furnaces, provided extra storage space, and doubled as storm shelters. Therefore, if we didn't have a basement, the house standing in a storm was not exactly irrelevant.

There was no garage and the land was wide open to the wind. That would make starting the car in winter a cold, nasty experience, but we thought we could tough it out until summer and then add a garage.

It was a typical ranch home. There was a small, enclosed entry porch in front. From the porch, you entered the living room. It had a huge picture window that faced the country road and beyond that a pasture full of horses. The view faced west and was wonderfully picturesque and serene.

There was a country-style kitchen, one medium bedroom, two small bedrooms, one bath, and a tiny utility room for the washer, dryer, and furnace. Certainly not a luxurious house, but a step up from our old one. Or so we thought. A wall with a window separated the living room from one bedroom. It turned out the bedroom had been added on to the original house, so there was actually an outside wall between them. The living room was paneled in dark wood on one end. Patterned concrete blocks separated the living room from the hall.

Even interior walls were concrete. I found out, later, this makes it difficult to hang pictures, or anything else for that matter. Ever try to drive a nail into concrete? If you haven't, it goes like this. BOING! The nail bounces off.

Unless, of course, you are smart enough to know about masonry nails. Guess what? We didn't.

Did I mention this was an "unconventional" home? Did I mention how naïve we were about home construction, etc? If not, I'll mention it here. We were very, very naïve and uneducated about home construction.

There were a few "minor" problems which we were assured would be fixed as soon as spring arrived. I learned an important lesson with this purchase: Get any "promises" in writing and make sure there is a penalty clause included. That said, I'll continue.

It was late February. First problem, there were twelve concrete wall panels scattered in the yard. Remember their size? BIG! The developer we purchased the home from was also the man who designed the house. He had plans to market this type home. He was in the process of turning his farmland into a subdivision.

Back to the concrete panels. Even though they were huge, they didn't look particularly intimidating. However, they were partially buried by snow. The intimidation would come when the snow melted. He assured us he would remove the panels as soon as the ground hardened after the spring thaw. That seemed reasonable. After all, he put them there, he should know if he could get rid of them. Why did he put them there, you ask? Apparently, the plan was to build a barn, and he changed his mind. The concrete slab for the barn floor had been poured at the end of the driveway. It was very, very big.

Second problem, the country road in front of our house was a private road that led to the main highway. That meant the road crew would not plow our road until all other roads in the county were cleared. Private roads were always plowed last. We were young. We were foolish. We were trusting. We were not too bright. And, we were adventurous. So we decided, in our ignorance, none of this was important. First, last, what difference? Let me clarify something. Last can make a huge difference! I wasn't pleased with that position in the show ring or in any competition, so why was I accepting of it in a snowstorm? How many roads, do you suppose, were in that county? That was a question I should have asked because, if you're last in a line of two, it might be okay. But, if you're last in line of, say...lots and lots...it can complicate your life.

Other questions come to mind if you have a mind that works. For example, how many miles long is each road? And, how long does it take to plow a road? We learned the answers to those questions. 1) The county had many, many roads to plow. 2) County roads were miles long. 3) The time it takes to plow one road depends upon the depth of the snow, how much drifting the wind has caused and, you guessed it, how many miles long the road is. See what experience has taught me? I now know what questions to ask. Too bad I didn't know in the old days.

Mr. Developer just glossed over the fact that the road had a few major potholes in it. He promised that, in a year or two, the road would be paved. Anyone with a lick of sense knows you get that kind of thing in writing! We did not have a lick of sense and were way too trusting. There were two other homes up the hill from us and our developer assured us that, after he sold a few more lots, he would have the cash to pave the road. In the meantime, we could just drive around the holes. It wasn't as if there was any traffic coming or going. Well, he was right about that. No traffic. We decided his plans seemed reasonable and we could temporarily drive around the holes.

Third problem, the entire five acres was fenced with woven wire pasture fencing. While this is fine for animals, it looks a bit odd running in front of your house. Especially not esthetic were the huge, swinging wooden gates that allowed tractor and truck entrance to the property. Of course, the house had been built in the middle of a pasture. I guess they just shooed the critters out of it and plopped the house down without a thought to landscaping.

Solution? We could take down the fencing across the front of the lot and improve the landscaping. That sounded like a plan. However, this is one of those seemingly simple things that are not as simple as they appear. For those who do not live in farm country, let me educate you. The woven wire fence was attached, every ten feet, to large wood posts. First, you had to remove the thick wire staples that held the wire to the posts. These lethal little babies don't give up the fight easily. Even with a staple puller, it's a chore. Then, you pull off wire that had been in one position for years and try to roll it up. Remember the wire that wouldn't unroll? Well, it doesn't roll up all that easy, either.

Next, you remove posts that are buried two feet deep in dirt. Last, you dispose of said wire, staples, and posts. I won't describe the battle with two six-foot-wide gates. Let's just say the entire process is NOT simple! Take my word for this. At the time, however, we thought—no big deal. WRONG! It turned out to be a project that bonded husband and wife. Up until that time, I had never heard Bruce curse, and it added another dimension to our marriage.

Fourth problem, there was a seventy-five-foot driveway from the road to where a garage would be. Of course, there wasn't a garage, yet, but that's problem number five. Said driveway was rutted and needed a gravel fill or paving. Paving was very expensive. We opted for gravel, but would have to wait until—you guessed right—the ground hardened after the spring thaw. It never occurred to us to ask what would happen to the driveway when the spring thaw arrived. Oh, would you like an answer now? Your car sinks into the mud. Up to the hubcaps. Bruce was not happy when he lost our car this way, but the tow truck driver did get it out, so why all the nasty glares? Something about he was a city boy and expected cars to sit on top of driveways, not within them. Whine, whine, whine.

Problem number five, the lack of a garage. I decided no big deal, we would have one built. A nice big one. Bruce just rolled his eyes, disgustedly, when I suggested it would make a good do-it-yourself project. He drew a line in the sand and said no way was he going to build anything. Okay, okay. I did admit to him that there were people who built garages, and he wouldn't have to. He muttered something about, "Good call." I failed to mention, in order to save money, we would have to paint and do a few odds and ends, but I figured what he didn't know wouldn't cause him any sleepless nights. I was saving him mental anguish. What a great gal.

Problem number six, lack of dog facilities. We would have to start from scratch and put up kennels. And, there was no place to groom. Remember my grooming salon in the basement? I needed the same kind of setup here. While I didn't intend to stay in the dog grooming business, I had to groom my own dogs. I pondered, then got excited. I could solve both problems. I would design my own small kennel building, with grooming area, behind the barn's concrete slab which was problem number seven. The kennel building could have indoor/outdoor runs. I figured, if we put the garage in front of the concrete slab and the kennel behind the slab, we could run a fence between the buildings and have a complex of sorts. That meant the barn's concrete slab would be used and not become an eyesore. I thought it was an amazing idea.

Bruce wasn't so sure. I think the "fencing" thing gave him pause. After all, who were the people who were going to install the fence? I think he was having flashbacks to the fencing project in town. I knew we were going to have to do this ourselves. Our money was stretched to the limit. We could afford to add the buildings, but were going to have to do as much of the actual work as we could. I just glossed over that part and decided we could build a small kennel building and, in the future, add a tiny barn to the back. That way, I could actually have a horse! My lifetime dream! My own horse and a place to put it. Bruce paled, but didn't say no. You see, he didn't ride horses. He didn't even particularly like them at that point in his life. They were something cowboys rode and accountants stayed away from.

Problem number seven, the barn slab. I had eliminated this one with my awesome construction project.

Problem number eight, there were several very deep ruts in the yard beside and behind the house. Mr. Developer said a truck carrying concrete panels had gotten stuck and when it was towed out, small canyons were left behind. He assured us he would have the deep ruts filled in. The panels were extremely heavy and that's why the truck sunk into the ground. They wouldn't make the mistake again of driving a truck loaded with panels onto ground that was soft from rain. At least, they had learned something from the experience. After all, isn't that what life's all about? Learning? Too bad I take so long to learn everything.

That word "heavy" should have been a clue to problem twelve. That being, if the panels were so heavy, how was he going to get them out without another truck sinking into the ground? Would they have to wait until it stopped raining? And, how long does ground take to firm up after spring rains? And, does anyone know how much it rains in spring in Wisconsin?

Moving right along, he did explain that any moving of panels would have to wait until the "ground hardened after the spring thaw." He neglected to mention the "rain" thing. And, I never thought about what had happened under the concrete panels, what might be living under there, the condition of the ground, and exactly how far down did they sink? Mr. Developer didn't divulge that information, if he knew, which I would like to think he didn't.

Problem number nine, there was an orchard in front of the house. Mr. Developer said the trees would need occasional pruning, but nothing else. They were miniature fruit trees and looked quite nice, even without leaves or fruit. We were told we'd be able to enjoy all kinds of fruit. There were about thirty of these trees. When spring came, they looked great. They never, however, produced fruit of any kind. Not one morsel. They never grew taller either. I guess that's what "miniature" means. They just—sat there. I suppose that's okay. I mean, they were contributing oxygen to the Earth's atmosphere but, it seems to me, fruit trees should make fruit.

I tried various things. Fertilizers, extra water, and lovingly explaining in tree language that they needed to produce. But, in the end, it turned out whoever planted them only planted male trees and they don't make fruit! I mean, who knew that trees come in different genders? I didn't. Not until a friendly farmer told me. And, apparently, whoever planted them didn't, either. So, maybe I shouldn't have listed them under "problems." They weren't really a problem, more a mystery to be solved.

Problem ten, there was a fence that separated the two acres that the house sat on from the three acres behind it. This was good because that meant we already had a separate pasture in place. The fence needed painting. It looked shabby. We only have nine problems so what's one more? How much work can painting five acres of fencing entail? I mean, in most places it just meant painting the posts. There was only a few hundred feet that had boards to be painted. I assured Bruce that painting fence posts would be easy. You just swipe up and down and move on. The boards just require side to side. Easy.

As for the pasture itself? Meet problem number eleven. As I gazed upon it, I thought, taking care of the pasture won't be hard. You just let a pasture—pasture. It sits there and looks wonderful. There's that naïve streak showing again. Mr. Developer failed to mention that the pasture had been neglected for years. What that meant, folks, was rocks and weeds. Rocks that were never properly removed and weeds that were never—properly removed. Horses don't do well in pastures of rocks and weeds, and I intended to have a horse. But, it was winter and all looked serene. Problem number eleven wouldn't surface until late spring.

I later learned that keeping a proper pasture is a science! You need to rotate your animals so the grass doesn't get overgrazed. You need to plow up sections to renew the dirt and replant it. You need to carefully choose what kind of grass you're going to feed your animals. You need to fertilize tender grass shoots as they grow. You need to remove horse droppings. You need to move back to the city where grass is only a small part of your yard. Who knew simple grass could be so complicated!

There were other problems, but I'm getting tired of listing them, so we'll talk about them as they come up. I hope you're getting the idea by now. Our dream home never truly became a nightmare, but it certainly was a...challenge.

At this stage of my life, as I write this, I'm thinking, Did I have any brains at all? Did I have a lick of sense? Why was I born overconfident and sure I could solve any problem? I'm sure Bruce is asking himself the same questions.

We enthusiastically bought the house, confident the problems were simple and easily fixed. At least, I was enthusiastic. Bruce seemed to have a permanent grimace on his face.

You see what's happening? We bought a puppy. Now we have a pack of dogs, have to move to the house from...heck...and still don't realize we're on a slippery path leading to...what? Hmmm. It's probably a good thing we didn't know where we were headed, but we were being educated getting there.

Oh, and we need a bigger vehicle to transport our growing pack. So, we bought a van. Of course, we didn't have the van when we moved because we had to order it and it would be delivered "sometime after the spring thaw." What was it with the "after the spring thaw" thing? Having that vehicle would have simplified our moving. But, as you can see, "simplified" was not destined to be part of our lives.

We were scheduled to move the end of March and take delivery of our van in April. We were happily excited about all our new projects. At least, I was. I'm not sure Bruce was. Every family has a realist, and Bruce is ours. Movers and shakers (Kathy) are always enthusiastic. Realists (Bruce) deal with the problems movers and shakers cause.

In addition to all the upcoming projects, the move meant that Bruce's commute to work went from five minutes to thirty. Not a big deal? Not in summer, but it can be in winter when the roads are icy and you're sliding to and fro through intersections. That thirty minutes can easily turn into a hair-raising hour of adventurous driving. Do you really think Bruce needed more adventure in his life? He chose accounting because it fit his personality and skills. I think what he incorrectly chose might have been his wife.

The day of our move came. It was cold and gloomy. Things went fairly smoothly until Sheri was dragged down the hill in front of our house and skinned up a bit. The Siberian she was taking to the car got excited at the prospect of a car ride and charged downward. Sheri never let go of a leash in her entire life, not even at the age of eleven. As the Siberian bolted, she hung on, lost her footing, and, well...I took care of her boo-boos and tears. I'm not sure I soothed her injured pride, however. The trip downhill was not pleasant to watch. Legs, arms, dog and Sheri bodies were flying in all directions—not a ladylike descent in any way. She exhibited all the grace of her mother flopping down on the golf course. The trouble with owning sled dogs is, when you fall down and they feel weight against the collar, they lean in and pull. Result? You can be dragged a very long way even if you're screaming at the top of your lungs. Again, I speak from experience.

The movers had a hard time fitting everything into the new house. I thought we had increased our space. I never thought to measure and compare square footage. I didn't realize how much stuff we had in the blasted basement that we no longer had. Plus, I hadn't factored in the huge attic we had loaded with more stuff. The new house didn't have an attic. When the movers left, we had wall-to-wall boxes and furniture. There was barely a path leading from room to room. What a disaster! Oh, well. It certainly was incentive to downsize. Here's some advice from me to you. Downsize before you move. It's easier that way.

At that point, it started to rain and my three Siberians were tied outside. We were not going to put up our chain-link kennel as we had made arrangements for builders to begin the kennel and garage construction in the following weeks. So, the plan was to stake the dogs out on chains next to their doghouses. Oh, yes. We had acquired a new doghouse for Baku. This would be a very short-term situation. And, as much as I hated tying up my dogs, there was no other way. We contemplated putting up the old kennel run on the existing slab, but decided it wouldn't be sturdy enough. The kennel at our old house had been secured by short pipes embedded in the concrete into which the kennel panel legs fit. Therefore, the panels were not in danger of tipping or collapsing. That wouldn't be the case with a freestanding kennel, so we opted not to take a chance of it coming down.

So, my babies were outside in the rain on grass. I freaked because they would get muddy. I worried that they wouldn't have sense enough to go into the doghouses. Brandie and Natasha never used the blasted things and this was Baku's first experience with one. I contemplated showing him how to use it and decided sitting in a doghouse with a wet Siberian in thirty-some degree weather was not going to happen. I was too grumpy from the move to be a good companion for him. Besides, with my winter coat and boots on, I might get into the doghouse, but getting out could prove impossible.

I was stressing because I could hardly walk through the house. I had miscalculated the amount of our stuff and the new house's size. And, I was stressing because it was now pouring rain and my dogs were chained outside. Bringing the dogs inside certainly wasn't an option unless they could be stacked on top a box.

Bruce convinced me that Brandie, Natasha, and Baku would be just fine. I had this fear they would drown in the rain, get stuck in the mud, or somehow escape and disappear into the countryside forever. After all, it was much darker in the country, with no streetlights, than it had been at home. I couldn't even see the dogs from our window and was sure they were gone. It took weeks to get used to the pitch black of the country nighttime.

The other dire possibility was my beloved dogs would die in the elements. It seemed to me that the weather must be harsher out in the country. Especially, because we were not protected by houses and more exposed to the wind. But, I must admit it was warmer than it had been all winter and the only difference was the dogs were chained to doghouses instead of in a chain-link kennel. I didn't like the idea of their little paws getting dirty when they had always been clean on concrete, but there wasn't much I could do about it.

Bruce was stressing because he couldn't believe I had talked him into this mess.

We went to bed exhausted. I woke up early and rushed to look out the kitchen picture window that faced the backyard to check on my dogs. They were gone! Vanished! Rain had turned to sleet overnight. Everything was layered with a coat of thick ice. There had, obviously, been an ice storm. We were without electricity.

Okay, don't panic! They're probably in the doghouses.

I never thought about the fact that nothing in our house worked. All I could think about was my dead critters. I threw on a coat and boots and charged outside. As I approached the doghouses, my panic grew. The dogs weren't gone. They were laying, unmoving, outside of their houses under a layer of ice. My heart dropped. They were dead. I just knew it. Some owner. Some mother. I moved them to the country so they could have more room to romp and I killed them!

As I ran to my dead Baku, he raised his head and yawned.

It's a miracle! The dead have been raised!

When I started talking to him, he stood, stretched, shook off the ice, wagged his tail, and smiled at me. Brandie and Natasha came to life and did the same things. I realized the idiots had chosen to lay out in the rain and ice rather than go into their snuggly warm, safe doghouses.

I checked each one over carefully. They seemed happy and content. I checked their skin. Not wet. The husky coat had kept them completely dry. They bounced up and down happily and seemed thrilled with their new digs. They even added happy rollovers and nose plows through the icy grass. I went into the house to recover.

Incidentally, this behavior continued the entire time we had our Siberians. They loved cold, wet, snowy weather. That shouldn't have been surprising. After all, they are bred to survive in those conditions. However, I always found it nerve wracking. I wanted them dry and clean. They preferred wet, soggy, and sloshing through the muck or snow.

I trudged into the house and realized it was cold inside as well as outdoors. The dogs were happy and safe, so it was time to deal with the humans' discomfort. We had never lost power in the city, so this was a new, undesirable experience. Power down in the country means no water because well pumps don't work, in addition to no lights, no stove, no furnace, no appliances of any kind. The house was chilly, but not terrible. Our concrete walls kept the house insulated. And, I guess if you factor in all those boxes lining the walls, you have some kind of super insulation. It was a trifle cumbersome wearing coats in the house, but, at least it wasn't cold enough to see your breath. That's how Wisconsinites determine the severity of winter. If you can't see your breath and your nostrils don't stick together, it's not all that cold.

We had some food for the day, but nothing for dinner that didn't need cooking. My plan had been to shop for groceries the next day. So, we decided to go into the nearest small town and eat at a restaurant. Bruce drove carefully on icy roads. He skillfully drove around all the fallen tree limbs and downed electrical wires that were still coated with ice. It was amazing to see big power wires snaking across the road. It did make it a bit of a challenge to drive around them. But, we weren't frightened in any way, just in awe. This is where the "common sense" thing comes into play. You see...we should have been frightened! You don't drive around power lines! Egad! Did we own a brain between us?

We naïvely drove around wires and calmly assumed that, once we got to town, the electricity would be on. We were right. It turned out there was only one restaurant open and it only had a few customers. We found out why from the one waitress who was shocked when we told her where we lived. A state of emergency had been declared because of the horrible weather conditions. No one from the outlying areas was supposed to be out of their homes. It was way too dangerous to be driving on the roads. Uh-oh. Can you be arrested for "state of emergency" if you break or ignore it? We weren't sure.

We decided if we were going to be arrested, we might as well have it happen on a full stomach. So, we sat down and ordered. Then, we slinked out and waited for sirens to wail on our way home. I guess the deputies that patrolled that area had their hands full, so we were not detected as we wound around power lines and skidded back home. We later found out why a state of emergency had been enacted. It was because ice-coated power lines and limbs had broken under the weight creating all kinds of hazards. There were vast numbers of downed power lines. Many of them were still "hot" as power company crews were stretched to their limits. I don't think I need to tell you what "hot wires" mean. Suffice to say "hot wires" electrocute you and we were skidding around them. Plus, factor in the danger of an ice-coated tree falling on you and "state of emergency" meant STAY HOME! Do guardian angels stress out?

We were without power overnight and, when morning dawned, a few inches of snow had fallen. I had enrolled the children in local schools before we moved and was told the school bus would pick them up down on the main road. Jason was in first grade and Sheri in sixth grade. Just to be sure everything was in order, I called the school to make sure they were on the schedule for pickup. I was told they were and I asked what I had to do. The woman chuckled and said, "Just have the children wait on the main highway by the mailboxes."

Excuse me! These are my precious offspring. I don't leave them standing anywhere! Shouldn't they have a flag or a placard or a pass or something? How is the bus driver going to know who they are? What if the bus driver thinks they're hitchhikers and zooms past? How will I know if they're on the right bus? Precisely what time was the bus going to get there? And, how was I going to know when they were dropped off? What if...

The woman laughed and said bus drivers know what they're doing. There was only one bus on that route, so the kids couldn't get on the wrong one. As for pick up time? Sometime between 8:00 and 8:30. As for drop off time? That depended on the condition of the roads. School was dismissed at 3:00, so it would be after that.

I'm thinking, hah! So you say, lady! I want to see that bus driver's credentials! I want to be sure my kids are going where I think they're going! And, I want a more precise timetable than that, both coming and going!

I was really annoyed with this obvious slipshod way of doing things. So, I decided to wait with the kids and grill the bus driver to make darn sure he knew his stuff! We had about a two-block walk to the main road. It was cold and...you guessed it...the private road in front of our house wasn't plowed, so it was slippery walking. I had watched Bruce slip and slide down the road when he drove off for work and expected a whining session when he got home but, hey! He made it! Of course, me walking on it was another story. Why isn't this road properly taken care of? A woman could fall down! Especially one with my history of klutziness.

We stood, waiting, by the mailboxes. It was cold and blustery. I gazed down the lonely stretch of road. There wasn't a car or person in sight. We were completely alone in a sea of white. The desolate, surrounding fields were covered in snow. Blowing wind swirled across the land. Hardened snow crunched under our boots and was the only sound, other than the creaking wind. I had never felt so isolated. It was eerie and disquieting.

After what seemed like an eternity, a small yellow object appeared, stopped a few times, then grew larger and came to a lumbering halt in front of us.

The driver had passed the first test. He showed up and stopped.

The door opened. He said, "Hi," and gestured the kids in. I started to ask a question and the door shut in my face. The bus lumbered off. Hey! Get back here! Where are your credentials!

I was left standing in the freezing cold, a question frozen on my lips.

My babies! Bus, get back here!

I panicked. I ran...okay, I stumbled, skittered, and slid...back to the house, grabbed my purse, prepared to jump into the car, then remembered we only had one car, and Bruce took it to work.

I called the school secretary and reported that I wasn't sure my kids had gotten on the right bus. She asked where we lived and, when I told her, she said, "Oh, yes. Mrs. Boettcher. I talked to you a little while ago. Remember? There's only one bus on that route. It stops first at the grade school, then comes here. If you saw them get on the bus, then that's where they are. They'll be dropped off at the right schools."

Good grief! That doesn't help any! That means I have to take your word for it and I don't know you! I need proof!

Jason was attending a small country grade school. Sheri was in sixth grade, and the East Troy Middle School was sixth, seventh, and eighth. I was already nervous about my sixth grader being put in with high schoolers. In Waukesha, Jason and Sheri had attended the same grade school and that always made me feel confident they were both safe. It was traumatic enough having them separated, but this bus thing was totally unnerving!

I was not reassured, but there wasn't much I could do. She sounded cheery and confident, so I finally decided I had to take her word. But, if my kids did not come home, I would hunt her down and deal with that cheery, confident voice!

But, how would Sheri and Jason know which bus to take home? Oh, my goodness! Who knows where my kids will end up.

I would be told, later that night, disdainfully, by my unappreciative offspring, that each bus had a number on its side for identification, and they were smart enough to find their bus!

As I stood by the kitchen window, contemplating life without kids, I realized I could see where they would be dropped off because the field between our house and the road was empty. From 3:00 on, I hovered at that window until I saw the bus lumber to a halt and my kids cross the road headed toward the house. I breathed a sigh of relief, and thanked God they were okay.

It's amazing how time and experience changes us. Within a few days, I was no longer walking them to the bus stop, I was watching from the window. Within a week or two, I had the approximate times of pickup and delivery down pat and watched from the window at that time. I realized the school and drivers did know what they were doing, were completely reliable and trustworthy, and didn't need advice from a neurotic city person. I never worried again.

Within a few weeks, the snow had melted and spring was beginning to emerge. Temperatures were warming. There were sprigs of green peeking up through brown, dead grass. Birds' chirping punctuated the quiet air.

I had unpacked, thrown a great deal away, and had some semblance of order.

A new burning-barrel, actually an old oil drum, was delivered. In those days, in the country, there was no trash pickup. We were told that what didn't burn had to be taken to the dump. Dump? What's a dump? We have to drive where and "dump" what? Drag stinky stuff with us and do what with it? Oh, yuck! That's icky work. Where are the strong guys who drive up to your house in the big truck and haul stuff away? Not here, apparently.

The Golden Guernsey Dairy guy drove up and told me I was on his delivery route. I thought, how neat! He brings dairy products right to the door. I signed up, got a spiffy metal box to put on the porch, and was given an order form. He said, "Just put the order form in the box on Tuesdays and Thursdays and I leave whatever you want. The bill will be left once a month."

That was great! I lost the trash guy, but gained a dairy guy. However, I discovered you do have to remember to fill out the order form or you get whatever the dairy man thinks you need. You also have to remember to take the stuff out of the box because it spoils after a day or two in the warm sun. I especially loved ordering delicious ice cream. This is where the...you have to remember to take the stuff out of the box...comes into play. Over time, I lost many items to the unrelenting sun. True, the milkbox was insulated, but my memory was not.

One morning, I suddenly remembered I had forgotten to retrieve my order. I raced to the box and picked out a soggy half gallon of ice cream. As I hurried to the kitchen, the bottom dropped out of the carton and a square of ice cream hit the carpet. I stared at the frozen treat, sighed, went to the kitchen, grabbed three spoons, and called the kids. We hadn't had breakfast yet, but who cared? We sat on the floor and spooned ice cream into our mouths. Conscious of germs and bacteria, I told them only to eat the top layer. We finished off our breakfast. I went outside, rounded up several of our dogs, brought them in, and watched as they enthusiastically licked the bottom layer of ice cream decorating my carpet. When they finished, all I had to do was take a wet cloth over the carpet. Another crisis solved by Kathy!

About this time, Bruce had a run-in with our driveway. I suppose that sounds odd—a run-in. But, that's really what happened. After a few days of drenching rain, he drove onto its dirt surface and literally—ran into it. Or, maybe I should say sunk into it. Like in—up to his precious hubcaps. And also up to his ankles when he got out of the vehicle. He stepped out of the car and his feet disappeared into Mother Earth.

My, my, all that ranting over a little mud on the shoes, pants, hubcaps, and briefcase. (He dropped it while trying to dislodge his shoes.) Did you know that mud can suck your shoes right off your feet? I didn't. But, after that little episode, I did. So, let's include socks in the list of Bruce's mud things.

The solution was fairly simple. That is, after we had the car towed out of the driveway. We needed to fill in the driveway with gravel. I ordered a load. The gravel company spread it down the length of the driveway. Oh, dear. All that gravel didn't seem to make much of a difference.

After driving on it for a few days, the gravel disappeared into the mud. We ordered another truckload. A few days later, we ordered another truckload. Bruce wasn't amused when I told him there was a gravel troll hiding in the mud spending his nights sucking rocks into his own personal quarry. I thought that was fairly amusing.

However, he was paying the bills and his sense of humor was lost somewhere between pages 14 and 15 of the checkbook register.

I don't remember how many truckloads of gravel it took to put a hard surface on the driveway. Let's just say—more than a few.

Our new van was delivered. What excitement! It was huge. We had our very own Chevy van for dog crates, critters, supplies, and kids. It was a top-of-the-line vehicle. Sheri and Jason were grateful they no longer had to share a back seat with squirming dogs. We were so proud of that van. It was two-tone green and we had vanity plates made that read "BRUKA." We felt official and competent. Of course, now we needed three large crates in which to transport the Siberians. See how things continue to mushroom?

I was now training Baku in addition to Brandie and Natasha. Frosty was temporarily retired from classes. I had tried another "fun" match and been thoroughly humiliated by his antics. Although he was a crowd pleaser, my ego couldn't take that kind of "restructuring."

Bruce really enjoyed driving the van. I, on the other hand, found its length and width a challenge. Factor in my ridiculous habit of backing too fast down our long driveway and an "incident" was in the making. Bruce warned me about the speed at which I backed up. I ignored him. After all, there was no traffic in our driveway, I was in a hurry most of the time, and what did he know?

I was complaining about a problem we were having with the two gigantic gates that sat at the entrance of the driveway. They would swing open and shut in the wind even though we had put concrete blocks in front of them.

We had decided to pull down the entire length of fence along our front property line but, so far, hadn't started it. I did the—"I've got an idea. We can do it ourselves. How hard can it be? It's easy. It'll be simple," routine. We set aside a Saturday and spent the day struggling to remove wire from posts. Hours of work and we made little headway. We decided my idea was "idiotic," we couldn't "do it ourselves," and not only was it "hard," it wasn't going to happen without help from someone who knew what they were doing and had some equipment. What kind of equipment we didn't know, but figured the "expert" would. Know, that is. We left wire dangling from posts and started checking the local newspaper for a handy person.

Back to the dancing gates. I'll set the scene. It was a blustery, rainy day. I was in a hurry. I jumped in the van, glanced over my shoulder, noticed the gates were open and, in my usual, reckless way, floored it. The van raced backward and...whumpppp! Oh, what a sickening sound. No, I didn't crash into the gate. Remember, I said they were open. I did a much trickier maneuver. It seems one gate was swinging shut as I approached. It was actually parallel to the van. Somehow, I managed to back alongside the gate, catching it on the side-view mirror. Did you know that a huge, wooden gate that is jammed against a side-view mirror will buckle a door inward? Bruce was not amused when I pointed out that I had collapsed the door without scratching anything. And did he realize how difficult it was to "impale" a gate that way?

What is it with men and their vehicles? If I had been buckled inward, would he have even noticed? I doubt it. And, the van didn't cost all that much to fix.

By May, our lawn was growing. Fast. Tall. Taller than I would have thought possible. Bruce tried mowing it with our small city power mower. Back and forth, back and forth, back and forth. The blasted mower was too narrow. We figured out we needed a much bigger mower. Much, much bigger! We went shopping and tried to find something that could do the job without taking a year. We truly had not realized what a big job mowing that yard would be. We finally ended up buying a riding 16 horsepower tractor complete with removable mower and snow blower. That seemed to take care of two problems. However, when they said "removable," they didn't say "easy." But that was next winter's lesson.

The tractor was delivered late one afternoon. Man, I loved riding that tractor! What fun! I wanted to mow the grass right away because it was knee-high by this time. Now, I admit Bruce warned me not to cut the grass in the morning, because it would be wet. Before it was mowed, the grass needed to dry in the sun from morning dew. And, he lectured that he knew I was itching to cut grass, but to wait until he got home because I might get hurt. Hurt? Me? Ridiculous! I understood how to drive the tractor. You just start the engine, listen to it purr, engage the mower, and...drive!

I watched him leave for work in the morning, did my morning chores, and stood looking at the tractor. Then, I sat on the tractor. Then, I revved it up and drove up and down the driveway. I eyed the tall grass and thought, I'll surprise Bruce. When he comes home, the grass will be cut!

I engaged the mower, confidently drove into the grass, went down the length of our lot and...fire! Fire! Smoke was coming from the engine! Fire!

I turned it off, ran for the hose, remembered we didn't have a hose, and ran back. There wasn't a fire. Hmm. Why all the smoke?

I tried again. It started okay. Oh, well. Tractors must have some sort of break-in period. Maybe they smoke like some new electric pots and pans. I shrugged and decided, maybe, all new tractors smoke that way. Again, I drove into the thick grass.

Oh, no! More smoke!

I shut the thing off and decided it was defective. When Bruce came home, I told him we had a defective tractor. He said we didn't have a defective tractor—he had a defective wife! That statement seemed rather harsh.

He lectured you can't drive a mower through wet, thick grass. Something about, if the grass is thick and high, it needs to be dry. And on and on and on and on. Bruce tersely explained to me, through gritted teeth, that I had burned out the belts. I swear to you, it was not a big deal. Belts aren't that expensive. Okay, installing them can be tough if you've never done it before. But, think about what we learned how to do. Of course, I got the—"I am a CPA, I don't need to learn how to do tractor belts,"—dissertation, but I firmly believe the more knowledge we acquire in this life, the better. Apparently, Mr. CPA didn't share that philosophy.

Okay, I admit he might have been right about the wet grass thing. Once the grass was dry, our new tractor-mower went right through it, and we had a manicured yard.

Remember me telling you about the ditch in the backyard? The one caused by the truck tire? I was really getting into the "mowing" thing. I mowed and mowed. I loved driving around in the fresh air and sunshine. However, it really bugged me that grass was growing up from that ditch and was standing taller than the ditch, waving in the wind. I mentioned it to Bruce and he said, "Who cares? It's in the backyard, no one can see it, and eventually, we'll fill in the ditch with dirt."

Eventually? That word wasn't even in my vocabulary. Can't he see that tall, askew grass is ruining our landscaping? I studied the ditch. I concluded that if I drove the tractor over the ditch and straddled it, the mower blade would level the grass. I measured the tractor's width and saw that, if I drove slowly and carefully, I could keep one tire on each side of the ditch. I figured that an inch of tire on each side would keep me out of the ditch.

Guess what? I figured wrong. I drove over the ditch and smiled, smugly, as the mower's blade leveled the grass. I wasn't smiling when the tractor tipped to the side and skidded into the ditch, its blade whump-whumping into the dirt.

I tried pushing the stupid tractor out of the ditch. I tugged, I pushed, I sighed, and then in defeat, braced myself for the lecture.

Bruce just shook his head when I showed him our new, half-buried tractor. I guess he was getting tired of lecturing. Seeing as how I was getting tired of hearing it, his silence was refreshing.

I told him the ditch monster reached up, pulled us in, and tried to gobble up the tractor, that I had escaped with my life and he should be happy I wasn't maimed with ditch monster claw marks. He didn't buy it and, definitely, wasn't amused. What a grumpy Gus. The story seemed plausible to me and even humorous in spots.

Okay, it took several hours to get the dumb tractor out of the ditch. We managed to use some old boards and lever the tractor upward until I could drive it out. Did I say we? All right, all right. Bruce levered it up. Darn. He always gets the fun part.

It was now June and everything was green, including our pasture. I was so focused on the front two acres, I had neglected the back three. It really didn't make any difference. We weren't planning on using the pasture for the time being. I did notice that beautiful purple flowers were growing back there. I felt really proud because that proved I could grow things. I could see the flowers were very tall, but didn't think much about it. That is, until a terrible windstorm blew the kids' plastic pool into the pasture. Bruce went after it and disappeared into the flowers.

Wow! Those things are really tall! Taller than Bruce. What the devil are they?

When he emerged, he grumbled that the pasture was like a jungle. We decided we'd better mow it. When we examined the stalks, we found they were very thick. What exactly were we growing?

We tried using a hand scythe. That's backbreaking work! And, much to our dismay, the blade either only partially cut through or just bounced off the flower's stalks.

Next solution: Bruce rented a gas-powered machine that had a long cutting blade. He managed to almost get around the perimeter of the pasture before the thing burned out. He had hardly made a dent in our crop.

We went back into the house and were discussing our problem, when a farmer drove by on his tractor. A light bulb went off in Bruce's head and he raced outside, talked to the farmer, and got him to agree to check out the pasture and mow it. You see, attached to his tractor was a huge mower with one long blade. I told Mr. Farmer that I loved the flowers, but thought they might be getting too tall. When we took him back to the pasture, his mouth dropped open, then he started to laugh. He said we were growing thistle. It's a noxious weed. Actually, in those days it was illegal to grow, because when it went to seed, the seeds would blow into cornfields, take over, and obliterate the corn. Mr. Farmer said we would be fined by the county if we didn't get that stuff out—fast!

So much for my florist days. Cutting that stuff proved to be an arduous task. Mr. Farmer said he had never seen thistle get that big and even he didn't realize how thick the stalks could be. I remember seeing him on his tractor. He would be smiling and shaking his head. It took him several days to cut and get rid of my beautiful thistle. Oh, well.

I was sitting on the sofa, planning my next project—a garden—when I looked up and saw a plane heading straight for our picture window. Our property was on a slight upward slope. The plane had come out of the west and was zooming over the neighbor's pasture. Horses scattered in all directions, galloping away at the sound of the buzzing plane. The plane was only a few feet off the ground and looked like it was going to hit our house. I shrieked and ran out the back door as the plane skimmed the rooftop, lifted upward slightly, and swooped over the cornfield behind our pasture.

I caught my breath and realized it was a crop duster. Let me tell you, those guys fly really low. Really, really low. It always unnerved me when they took a bead on that pasture and zoomed towards us. It seems they used our house as a landmark and, I swear, on more than one occasion I thought we'd have pilot guests and plane parts for dinner. However, it was amusing to watch visitors' reactions as they gazed out the picture window framing the oncoming plane and ran shrieking in all directions.

Now that the thistle was gone, I decided to keep the pasture mowed. Bruce absolutely forbade me from using his precious tractor because of rocks hidden underneath the grass and weeds. I pouted, then decided I would do it myself and didn't need his dumb tractor. I wanted that pasture manicured, and I wanted it done now. So, I spent weeks mowing with the small power mower we used for the yard's trim. I worked a little bit every day, moved rocks, and mowed the cleared spot. Finally, by fall, I had a lovely pasture. Hmm. I know what that lovely pasture needs! A horse or two! That can be my next project.

Perhaps I'd better take care of my current project first. I had planted the garden full of tomatoes, peppers, carrots, and a few other packages of stuff. But, up to now, it looked weird. Something seemed to be nibbling on my produce, and my rows weren't straight anymore. My mom, a terrific gardener, came out to see what my problem was. She looked at the garden and her eyebrows shot up. She was horrified just because I hadn't done any weeding. Weeding? What's that? You have to do what? I don't think so! That takes too much time and I'll get dirt under my polished fingernails, Mom. Besides, how do I know which is the weeds and which is the veggies? They all look the same to me. And, I'll get my knees dirty. I thought all I had to do was plant the stuff and it grew.

I got lectured about gardens and their proper care. Boy, oh, boy. I shut Bruce down and now I have to deal with Mom. Why is everybody against me?

After Mom left, I made a decision. It seemed to me that the creatures of nature needed the produce worse than I did. After all, I could go to the market and buy what I needed. They had to take what they could get. Plus, they didn't care if there were weeds. They seemed to find the good stuff just fine. Weeding wasn't the way I wanted to spend my days, so I graciously offered my garden to nature's little creatures and abandoned it to grow on its own.

There was only one problem with that. Some of the creatures, enjoying the gourmet feast, were gophers. And, when they discovered the bounty of food the city girl had left in their midst, they started to colonize. Here's a fact I didn't know. Gophers dig tunnels. Long tunnels. And, when you dig a tunnel, you need an entrance and an exit. Soon our yard was Gopher City.

I asked at the dog food store if they knew how to get rid of gophers. They sent me to the local feed store where I was shown traps and poison. Egad! I can't do either. If I do traps, I have to get rid of the gophers, and the feed store guy wasn't suggesting I send them on a cruise. He mentioned drowning. Oh, no! I can't drown the little guys. Poison? Absolutely not!

I pondered my dilemma as Gopher City grew and, one day while Frosty was romping in the yard, an idea popped into my head. Why hadn't I thought of it before? I had a varmint-chasing dog! I'll have him chase the critters away. Okay, there are a few flaws in this, but try to look at it from my naïve point of view. I never thought about what would happen after they were chased away. Gophers slinking back into the night didn't occur to me. I was focused on chasing.

I took Frosty to one of the holes, and he stood there wagging his tail at me. No, no, Frosty. I think you're supposed to bark and intimidate, not make friends.

I got down on my hands and knees to show him. I dug at the hole with my hands and made barking noises. I hoped the neighbors weren't watching.

Frosty thought the game was great. He wagged and licked my face. No, no, Frosty! We want to scare the daylights out of the gophers! Put your nose down there, get a whiff, and when one shows his face, terrify it and chase the thing away! This is how you earn your keep. Think about this. I know you've got chasing genes. Use them! Get on the scent!

I spent several hours with Frosty. Sheri and Jason tried to help. We diligently went from hole to hole. I showed Frosty how to dig, how to bark, how to...one moment. Why am I down here on my knees, sniffing in this hole? This is a dog's job!

Mr. Farmer happened by and asked what in blazes I was trying to do. I explained that Frosty was a varmint hunter, and we had a ton of varmints, but the blasted dog just didn't understand what he was supposed to be doing.

I could see Mr. Farmer trying not to laugh. I suppose the story was a trifle strange, and I did have filthy knees and hands and a few smudges of dirt on my face. I might have been hard to take seriously. He suggested we get a cat. Maybe several cats, keep them outdoors, and let them hunt.

Oh, great, just what we need. More critters. But, if it will keep the gopher population down, okay. Mr. Farmer said he had a mother cat and that I could have several of the kittens. He gave me three kittens that we bedded down in the small storage shed next to the house.

The next day, they were gone. At first, I thought they were catnapped, or taken hostage by the gophers but, when I told Mr. Farmer what had happened, he checked his barn. It seemed Momma cat had reclaimed her kittens overnight and taken them back to the farm. We brought the kittens back. Momma retrieved them. After several attempts at setting up our own cat-gopher hunting syndicate, we gave up. Momma cat had won.

Not to be deterred in the elimination of the gophers, I came up with another plan. Next stop, the drive-in restaurant on the way to town. I had seen a sign for kittens. We stopped by and picked up two babies. These guys decided our digs were just fine. We named one Tiger and the other Inky. The kittens loved us, the kids, and...the gophers. No, no! You're not supposed to become little friends with the gophers! Don't play with them!

Apparently, Inky and Tiger thought the furry little fellows were some kind of kindred spirits. It began to look as though our house was going to become an island in the middle of Gopher City. But, when Tiger turned six months old, he turned into a ferocious hunter, and the gopher population started to decline.

That was all well and good, until Tiger started bringing me his trophies. He would kill a gopher, and instead of disposing of the body in a civilized way, Tiger would chomp off the head and leave the body by the front door. Eewwww! Disgusting! Now I have to be a gopher mortician!

I was told by farmers that the body was a gift from Tiger. I guess he wanted me to acknowledge his handiwork. But, if he wanted to bring me a gift, how about candy or flowers? Scooping up headless corpses and giving them a decent funeral is not in my job description!

One morning, I was walking from the dog area to the backdoor in my usual daze, when something the size of a lion shot past me and under the porch. Okay, it wasn't that big, but my shrieking echoed through the air. It was furry, it was long, and it disappeared under the house! Help!

Bruce was at work, the kids at school. Help! There's a monster under the house! Calm down. You're alone, in the country where you've always wanted to be, in the middle of an overgrown garden, surrounded by gophers, and now, a monster's under the porch. Help! Hmm. No one's here to help. Guess I have to handle this myself.

I raced to the phone and called Bruce. Help!

He calmly asked me if I could see the creature. No.

Has it come back out? No.

What did it look like? Don't know. Furry.

What did I expect him to do? Ummm.

He said, "Don't worry, Frosty will protect you."

I really resented his laughing as he hung up. So much for manly defense of women. Looks like I'll have to be the manly hunter in this family.

I marched to the shed, grabbed a shovel, and carefully checked the back concrete porch with Frosty at my side. Hmm. Nothing. Oh, well. I guess I'm safe.

I turned to go back to the shed. Frosty started yapping. The chase was on! The creature ran lickety split across the yard with Frosty right behind and me chasing Frosty with my shovel. No, Frosty!

It occurred to me that, if Frosty caught the thing, it might fight back and what if Frosty lost the confrontation! I might have to whack the monster to death. Or, if Frosty won, I was going to have to get rid of it! Yipes!

Frosty, let it get away! Don't catch it! Forget all those lessons at the gopher hole! I don't care if you don't chase varmints! Come back here!

Oh, great. The dog finally decides to do what I taught him to do when I don't want him to remember what I taught him to do! Darn it! Stop! Come back!

Luckily, the creature zoomed across the road, disappeared into the horse pasture, and left a confused Frosty running back and forth, sniffing and yapping along the fence. I was later told that it was probably a mole. Mole? I thought that was a beauty mark on your face. This country stuff is a whole lot harder and scarier than I thought.

About that time, I started being attacked by birds. That's right. Just like in the Hitchcock movie. I would mow, and they would swoop down at me in flocks. Black birds swooping and diving. I was terrified as they took aim and dive-bombed me. But, I refused to abandon my super-duper tractor riding. How do you chase birds away? Hmmm. I think you swing at them. I know! I'll have Sheri sit on the back of the tractor and wave something at them.

I searched the house and decided the phone book might be big enough. I covered it in aluminum foil thinking the reflection might scare the birds, and...Yea! We had a magnificent bird shooer awayer. I thought Sheri's waving and swinging would keep them away from the tractor and we wouldn't be pecked. Sheri was an enthusiastic bird waver. She worked very hard as I mowed.

Apparently, the neighbors really enjoyed that show. However, after several mowing sessions, they took pity on me and explained that the birds were swallows. They weren't attacking me, they were dining on the mosquitoes my grass mowing was stirring up. I reassessed the swallows' attack patterns, and sure enough, they were diving in front and back of the mower. Hmm. A misjudgment on my part. To say I felt like an idiot is putting it mildly. I retired Sheri and the phonebook.

The ground finally hardened enough so the concrete panels could be removed. It took one entire day and was an amazing process to watch. However, it seems the ground wasn't all that hard because, when the final panel was hauled away, we had major yard work to do. There were truck tire marks to fill in with dirt. We tried smoothing out the gouges, but ended up ordering dirt to fill them in. And, no grass was growing under the deep depressions left by the panels. Only creepy, crawly, disgusting things were living there. Eeww! So, in addition to gouges, we had huge, deep bare spots filled with creepies building cities. That meant more filling and seeding. I told Bruce to look at the bright side. There were only twelve panels and twelve bare spots. From the way he glared at me, I got the idea he didn't think there was a "bright" side.

Also, you have to factor this into his discontent. The front fence had been taken down. The open space looked great, but the post holes needed to be filled in, and, you guessed it—seeded. I admit it took us a few weekends to accomplish all the filling and seeding, but who wants to spend weekends sitting in the house watching television when there's all that fresh air to enjoy?

In addition to all the chores, I was still going to my dog classes, and we were managing to attend dog shows. After all, we did have that big new van to carry everyone. Brandie and Natasha had picked up points towards their championships. Baku had won his share of puppy classes, and I was flying high. That's when Sheri decided she wanted to show dogs too. She began to watch Junior Showmanship at the AKC shows, decided that's what she was going to do, and worked on learning to show at the local conformation classes. She learned at an amazing rate. Sheri absolutely loved the dogs and the showing and never minded the work that went into training or taking care of them.

We entered her in an upcoming Iowa Kennel Club's Junior Showmanship competition. Sheri seemed to have a natural ability, welcomed constructive criticism, and for an eleven-year-old, had an unusual determined and intense talent for taking that criticism and applying it. It took only a few months for her to become as adept at handling dogs as I was after years of learning. She had her father's calm approach and truly appreciated the dogs as spirits with whom to cooperate, not bully. I loved watching her interact with her charges and still do to this day. I know from observing her that dogs and people can be loving, kindred spirits.

Jason also had, and has, that sense of oneness with animals. But, showing dogs was never his thing. However, he did try it. I think there was sibling rivalry going on. If Sheri could do it, Jason knew he could do it better. When he was seven, he and Sheri trained two beautiful red Siberian Husky puppies to be shown at a fun match. The puppies were in the two to four month class. Bruce and I beamed with pride as brother and sister entered the ring with gorgeous puppies that we had bred. What made it doubly exciting was that there were two fun matches being held at the same location. The puppies were entered in both. At the first fun match, Jason beat his sister and glowed and gloated as only a seven-year-old brother can.

However, at the second match, a different judge decided Sheri's puppy was the best, and she won the class. As the judge awarded Sheri her ribbon, the professional-looking woman smiled at the disappointed Jason and said, "Your puppy is nice too."

I know she was trying to lessen the blow of defeat. Jason looked truly miffed. Not defeated, Ms. Judge. Miffed. There is a difference.

Jason thought about it a moment, then looked the judge right in the eye and said, disdainfully, "No, my puppy isn't nice too. I know my puppy is better than Sheri's, because the other judge did a better job and gave me first place, not Sheri." He turned and left the ring.

I was stunned. So was the judge. So were the people watching. I wanted to apologize for what I considered to be rude behavior and went up to the judge after she left the ring. She laughed and said it was nice to know Jason was not afraid to state his opinion. That's what dog showing was all about. She was not offended in any way.

Jason, on the other hand, pouted for several days and could not be made to understand that both puppies were exceptional and the judge's opinion was the one that counted, not his. But, only in that moment on that day. That didn't make his opinion any less valid. He remained convinced the judge needed to be reeducated or needed better glasses. His analytical approach to life, backed by the courage to state his opinion, and his independent nature, were unusual attributes in a child of that age. And, while sometimes difficult to direct in a child, they are traits I'm proud of in the man. I always wanted my children to be independent thinkers. However, that can bite a Mom on the...whatever...when you're trying to direct a kid through childhood. I had to devise some rather unusual approaches to discipline as Jason grew to manhood. He'll tell you his Mom is just plain weird, and he's going to write an exposé to reveal his pathetic childhood. I prefer to think of myself a creative, innovative disciplinarian and always the winner of mother-son confrontations. He whines, much like his father, but there's a twinkle in his eye and a smile tugging at his mouth when he says the "Mom was just plain weird" thing.

Sheri also had, and has, an independent and courage-of-her-conviction streak. Hers showed up in the first show in Junior Showmanship. It was a hot, steamy summer day in Iowa. Sheri was in a class with twelve other Novice Junior Showmanship children. As we watched the judging with friends, we realized the competition was very tough. Those kids knew their stuff and were better handlers than most adults. For those of you who have never watched Junior Showmanship, it's different than judging dogs. The handlers' abilities are being judged, not the animal's conformation. In later years, I judged this class and was always amazed at the level of expertise these youngsters possessed. Many of them went on to become professional handlers.

The presentation, the dog's appearance, and the handler's appearance are judged. Then, instructions are given to determine if the kids are listening and can follow orders.

I remember thinking it didn't matter if Sheri lost because she looked so darn cute out there. She was wearing a blue dress with matching undershorts. Her little round face was bright red from working in the unrelenting sun. Her hair and face were wet from sweating. She was frowning in concentration and looked intense. She was adorable. Who cared if she won? She had the guts to compete. She was showing Natasha and had worked hard training the Siberian to stand perfectly. Take it from me, that was no small accomplishment. Natasha made me look like an idiot on numerous occasions—past, present, and future.

As we watched with a group of friends, I thought, That judge is going to have a rough time selecting a winner.

The kids were flawless.

The judge had them line up, then instructed the children to face her and the center of the ring. Kids quickly turned their dogs toward the judge and made sure they were standing properly. Then, the judge said something we couldn't hear. Eleven of the twelve entrants turned their dogs to the right. Sheri frowned, thought a moment, and turned Natasha the opposite way, putting her tail-to-tail with the dog who had been in front of Sheri. Sheri was at the end of the line, facing east. The rest of the class was facing west.

The audience gasped. My friend whispered, "Oh, no! What is Sheri thinking? That's a terrible mistake. Oh, Sheri, turn around!"

Sheri glanced over her shoulder at the rest of the class, studied them, scowled thoughtfully, and made a decision. She stayed right where she was.

After watching, the judge had the class turn back to face her before giving the instruction to gait the dogs around the ring.

My friends were commiserating with me over Sheri's faux pas. I was feeling sorry for Sheri and trying to decide what to say to her. The judge began to hand out the ribbons. She smiled at Sheri and gave her first place. It seems my independent daughter was the only one who followed directions correctly. The judge was trying to make a decision in a class where all things were equal, so she gave an unusual instruction and told the children to face left, thus showing the offside of the dog. That was not a move I had ever seen done in Junior Showmanship or the regular show ring. Apparently, neither had any of the Siberian people sitting with us.

At least, that's what we think she said. When we asked Sheri, she couldn't remember the instruction. I am curious to this day about what was said.

Needless to say, the Siberian Husky people were very impressed with Sheri's ability to follow a direction in a way she thought was proper, even though every other person in that class disagreed. I could not have been prouder of that child. I'm not sure I wouldn't have changed my mind in that situation.

Sheri went on to do a great deal of winning in Junior Showmanship. She qualified to compete in Junior Showmanship at the 1980 Westminster Kennel Club Show. We proudly watched her at Madison Square Garden where she competed with other Juniors and also showed two of our champions in the breed ring. It was an exciting experience.

Sheri has a great love of Terriers and Siberian Huskies. But, there's another breed that fills her heart with joy—the Alaskan Malamute. She has shown them almost as many times as Siberians. At age sixteen, Sheri was given an award by the Alaskan Malamute Club of America. She was the number one junior handler of Alaskan Malamutes in the United States that year. To say I'm extremely proud of her ability and love of dogs is an understatement.

On our minifarm, Bruce didn't complain too loudly as he filled in holes made by the concrete-panel-remover trucks, removed posts, and then seeded bare spots. There was a lot of muttering going on, but no discernible bad words. I should have stopped while I was ahead, but that's not something I'm known for. I heard an ad on the radio. It seems the State of Wisconsin Forest Service was giving away free pine trees if they were used as windbreaks. I gazed at our neighbor's house up the hill and envisioned this marvelous line of pine trees separating our properties. And, they were free! There was one small catch. You had to take one thousand trees. Bruce paled when I enthusiastically outlined our next project. He wanted to know who was going to dig the one thousand holes. I told him the trees would be very tiny, so they only needed a minor hole.

He wanted me to define—minor. I told him I would help. How hard could it be to dig some little holes?

I was annoyed he wasn't enthusiastically enjoying my vision. I suppose his vision was different from mine. It probably was of him digging holes, for eternity, as opposed to sitting in an easy chair watching a ballgame.

I really had no concept of one thousand holes. My CPA husband, whose career has always been about numbers, obviously did. But, he caved in, and we picked up our one thousand trees. Hmmm. Even one thousand tiny trees take up a bit of room. Oh, well. That's why we have a van. The trees were only six inches high and had tiny roots, so I just knew the digging would be easy.

First problem, how do you decide how close together to put one thousand trees so you don't have any trees left over? Bruce wanted to measure. Measure? That sounds boring and takes too much time. I want my trees planted right away. So, I know! Let's just guess.

Bruce's lips tightened. He insisted we were going to measure and figure this thing out. So we—I mean he—did. Measure, that is.

Next problem. We hadn't had much rain. The ground was fairly hard. Factor in the grass and its roots, and digging that tiny hole was too hard for me. So, we—I mean he—dug the holes.

It took a few hours longer than I had anticipated. Actually, it took hours and hours and hours. Okay, it took days and days and days. But, we—I mean—he—did it and we had a line of trees. Now, true, they were only a tad more than ankle high, but everyone knows pine trees grow tall, so the future looked great!

Mr. Farmer admired our trees and asked if we had watered them. Water them? Doesn't the rain do that? Yes, but there's no rain in the forecast. Uh-oh. The tree line is on the end of the property. We don't have a hose. Maybe it's time to get one. But it's several hundred feet from the house to that tree line, and it'll cost pretty much for enough hoses to reach that far. I know! Let's haul water to save money.

We hauled buckets and buckets and buckets of water, then, in our ignorance, assumed you only had to water them once.

Of course, that summer was one of the driest in Wisconsin history. The ground just sucked up the water, then turned hard. I'm not sure the pine tree roots ever got much of a drink. And, no one told us the trees had to be watered frequently. Hmm. Come to think about it, maybe that word "frequently" was used. But, exactly how frequent is—frequently? We weren't sure, so we hauled water now and then. In the end our trees died from thirst. So, I guess...now and then...wasn't frequently enough. All that work and no trees. It was very depressing when one day we discovered our pine trees weren't green, but an odd shade of brown. We gave them a proper funeral by mowing them down. It was a sad day as I chopped off one brown little stick after the other.

It gave me an appreciation for the work and plight of farmers. How many times do you read about crops failing for one reason or the other? I, for one, can relate. Farmers put their hearts, souls, money, and backs into planting and taking care of fields, then can be wiped out in a moment with a bad storm, or a season of drought, or a season of too much rain. I know personally the sinking feeling that comes with that experience.

Speaking of farmers, I never much thought about how they...farm. I learned a great deal living in the country. I would hear the tractors before daylight and see the tractor headlights late into the night during planting and harvesting seasons. The people I met were always friendly, glad to give advice, listened to your problems, and were wise in the ways of the land, animals, and human behavior. If you want to get in touch with homespun reality laced with genuine wisdom and sprinkled with a touch of humor, talk to farmers or their spouses. This is a recommendation from a city girl who grew to truly admire these folks.

It was summer and time to build our garage and kennel. I was so excited I could hardly stand it. I had labored over my plans and looked forward to the conference with the two guys who were going to do the construction. They came over one evening. We sat at the table, and I explained what I wanted done.

They looked at me like I had two heads and turned to Bruce, asking him what he wanted done. Now, you have to understand the times. It was the early seventies in Wisconsin. Men had certain ideas about women's place in life, our roles, and our duties. Apparently, designing a building was not listed in these particular two men's book of duties and chores for women.

I scowled and interrupted with my ideas and suggestions. They were condescending and the unspoken message was: Now, Kathy, let Bruce talk. This is man's work.

I was astounded and thought, One moment! I designed these buildings. I know what I want done and how I want it done! Let's talk to the architect here! That would be me!

No matter what I said, they talked around me. If they had been paying attention, they would have realized that Bruce was not answering their questions. He would look at me, and I answered. Yet, they continued to ask him everything. When they finally listened to what I wanted done, they shook their heads and ended our meeting by saying they didn't think my ideas would work.

I was devastated. I was certain the plans were workable. I could see the finished project in my head and really did understand about studs, boards, etc. My Dad was a skilled carpenter, and I had learned a great deal watching and helping him as a child. However, it was obvious these men were not going to listen to me, or even consider what I said as possible, so I devised a manipulative, diabolical plan. I convinced Bruce to be my front man. I would tell him what I wanted done. Then, he would relay that information to the construction guys.

We tried it out the next day. I prepared Bruce's script. He called the guys and explained the project again. When they were dealing with Bruce, suddenly the plans were workable.

They started the following week. Every night I would detail to Bruce what needed to be done next. He'd talk to our builders, and they would do what he said. It was quite amusing. If they had a question and I tried to answer it, they would say, "Have Bruce call us."

I would work out the problem, and Bruce would deliver the message.

As the buildings took shape, I was thrilled. My ideas were coming to life. I didn't care that Bruce was getting the credit because my dream was materializing!

My construction crew was awesome and obviously, knew their stuff. What they didn't know was that they were my construction crew.

One evening, as the project neared completion, there was a problem with the way the in/out doors in the kennel were offset. Mr. Builder told me about the problem. I offered a suggestion. He said I should talk to Bruce and let them know. Just as they were leaving, Bruce pulled onto the driveway.

Uh-oh! Bad timing! Mr. Builder was heading straight for Bruce. I hurried after him, thinking, How can I clue in Bruce?

Mr. Builder shook Bruce's hand, explained the problem, then asked what he wanted done. Bruce blinked a few times, pondered, hemmed and hawed, then looked me right in the eyes and said, "What do I want them to do?"

I kept my eyes on Bruce and answered, "You want them to...." And I told him what needed to be done.

I swear, Mr. Builder's jaw dropped as I explained every detail to Bruce.

Bruce smiled at Mr. Builder and said, without missing a beat, "I want you to..." Then, he repeated exactly what I had said.

Mr. Builder's eyes went from Bruce to me. He shook his head, smiled slightly, made eye contact with me, and said slowly, "You're the one calling the shots, aren't you?"

Like...duhhhh! Was anybody listening? I had been trying to tell them that from the beginning. Was I invisible? Hmmm. Here's a place for all sorts of rhetoric about women's struggle to be seen as equals—a place I could address many different ways to demand or elicit respect. Shall I get on a soapbox? It's tempting, but we'll talk about that some other time.

After that, I had no problem with Mr. Builder. I could see respect in his eyes as we worked together to finish our buildings. I had great respect for him from the beginning. Imagine being able to take boards, nails, and roofing, and create buildings. They took my dream, whacked boards into place, added a roof and siding, and turned that dream into a reality. What awesome talent!

Shortly before the garage was finished, Mr. Builder said we would have to paint the fourteen-foot-high overhang before he could put the finishing touches on the building. He needed it done by the next day. Bruce said he would do it when he got home from the office. I thought about it and decided I could take care of this. Bruce was spending every free moment doing something to our minifarm. I could, at least, paint. I offered. He said no. He did not want me up that high on a ladder with no one home. The ground around the garage was uneven and filled with rocks.

At first I thought, Great. I'll gladly let him do it.

I'm terrified of heights and fourteen feet up is high for a wuss like me. Then, there was...the ladder will have to be braced against the garage...thing. Exactly how safe is a "braced" ladder? Not safe enough when your knees are wobbling!

But, as I looked the project over, I decided maybe I could do it. I gathered my courage and left my brains in the house. I suppose there are some people who think you should keep your brains and wits about you at all times. They might be right.

I studied the building, then put the ladder up against it. The ladder wobbled under my weight as I climbed, then it started to slide to one side. Yipes! Let me off!

I scampered off just before the blasted thing clattered to the ground.

Okay, there might be a flaw in the way I had it braced. Try again.

I took a deep breath and put the ladder back up. This time I carefully checked the ground and made sure the ladder was braced. Then, I remembered that the first time I climbed I had forgotten the paint and brush. I guess climbing up to paint without the paint might defeat the entire purpose.

Oh, phooey! This paint bucket is heavy. And, how can I hold on for dear life with both hands plus carry the bucket and the brush? Answer? I can't.

Solution? Put the brush into the bucket, hold on with one hand, and slowly climb up. My heart thudded in my ears. I think it took ten minutes just to climb the dumb ladder. I was afraid to look down.

Okay, we're up here. Now what? You need the paintbrush. Oh, darn it! The stupid brush is up to the handle in paint. Hmm. Maybe that's okay because the more paint on the brush, the more I can slosh onto the trim. That way it shouldn't take too much time. I'll put the paint on nice and thick.

I only painted directly in front of my nose. Paint covered the trim, my hand, my clothes, the ladder, and when I climbed down weak-kneed, there were splatters of white on the ground. Maybe no one will notice. I mean, do you really look at the dirt under your feet? Not me.

It took me an entire afternoon just to do the trim on that garage. I would move the ladder a few feet, climb slowly, paint just what I could easily reach, wobble down slowly, and move. It was probably the slowest paint job in history.

I will admit I did fall one time. I only sprained my ankle. No big deal. I managed to wipe off the paint streak that ran from the trim down the entire length of the garage. I buried the puddle of paint on the ground with a pile of dirt. And, Bruce never noticed the garage had a tiny scratch where the ladder slid to the side. My bruises were hardly noticeable.

Plus, there was one other glitch. There I was, perched on the ladder, heart in my throat, when I heard Frosty barking frantically. Dumb me had left him outside to enjoy the weather and keep me company. I glanced toward the backyard.

"Frosty, no! No!"

My varmint chaser had finally figured out that chasing critters was fun. However, the critter he chased was Tiger the kitten. I saw a streak of gray, followed by a streak of white, zooming around the backyard.

Blast it! If he catches that kitten, he might hurt him!

"Frosty, stop it! Frosty, no! Frosty...."

The ladder was sliding to the side. To the sound of frantic barking, I tried to scurry down. I got a few feet from the ground when the ladder rapidly slipped sideways. I managed to jump to safety. However, do you know what happens when you jump with a bucket of paint? I'll tell you. It splooches! I was decorated with paint.

About that time, Tiger saved himself by scurrying up one of our clothes' posts. Frosty was jumping up and down, barking with fervor. I just stood there, eyes going from Frosty and Tiger to my newly decorated blouse. I must admit, I felt slightly defeated in that moment and had to quell an urge to kill Frosty by dunking him in the paint bucket. I took a deep, cleansing breath, trudged into the house, wiped paint off on a rag, picked up my camera, and trudged back outside. I don't know why I wanted to take a picture of Frosty and Tiger. Perhaps to immortalize the moment. The picture of Frosty jumping up at Tiger, high on the clothes' post, is in our family album.

I will admit I lied and told Bruce the paint job was simple and only took an hour. He was not happy that I had been foolish enough to climb so high and take a chance on falling.

Hmm. Should I tell him that I did fall and only was a smidge hurt? Then, I fell again and painted myself. And, that it was no big deal?

NOPE.

I shrugged off his little lecture. My guardian angels were probably in some bar belting back a few.

A few days later, our garage and kennel were complete! The garage was 2½ cars wide and wonderful. We could park both cars in it and were protected from the weather. There was the huge concrete slab behind the garage and then came our neat little kennel building. It had three dog runs that went in and out of the building. Each run had a 5′x5′ fenced inside area complete with gate and a 6′x12′ fenced outside area also with individual gates. There was a guillotine door in each run that could be closed to keep the dogs inside at night. During the day, they had free access in or out, depending upon their mood. I had added a long sloping roof that shaded all three runs. Part of the outside run was under cover and part was in open sun. We had bathing tubs and a grooming area inside, plus room for storing dog food. I had opted for making the inside chain link fencing only five feet high because it was open on top and my dogs weren't climbers. I proudly moved Brandie, Natasha, and Baku into their new digs. The setup was great—easy to clean and take care of. The dogs had plenty of room and would be protected from the elements, if I decided they needed to be, by shutting them in the building.

Hmmm. I stood back and had another brilliant idea. They needed a fenced yard in which to romp! If they romped several times every day, that would keep them in good spirits, healthy, and in good muscle for the show ring and sledding. If we lined the wood fence separating the pasture from the house yard with wire, then closed in one end and one length with a wire fence and surrounded the concrete slab between the garage and kennel with a picket fence, we'd have a dog complex! Let's see. How many pickets would we need? And...and how much wire do we need? Hmmm. Guess I need to use Bruce's measuring and figuring skills.

Then, there's that old problem about pounding in metal posts. I know! We'll dig holes and put in wood fence posts. They'll be stronger and more stable. And, to make sure they're stable, we'll pour some concrete in the holes and set the fence posts in the glop! Then, we can use those long, nasty staples to attach the wire to the posts. That should be almost indestructible with no wubbles. How brilliant! We can make the dog yard 200´ long and 100´ wide. Wow! Think of all the romping room!

I can still see Bruce sitting at the kitchen table, staring blankly out the window at the kennel, as I enthusiastically detailed my next project. I was envisioning the finished project, and my dogs romping playfully. I think he was envisioning his aching back, blistered hands, and possible escape to Tahiti. Actually, his hands had toughened up from the tree digging, and his back seemed okay to me.

Bruce did like the idea of the dogs being able to run. And, he enjoyed interacting with the incorrigible beasts, so he agreed.

Yea!!!! He's on board!

I called to order posts from the local lumberyard. Oh. You don't deliver? Okay. They'll fit in our van. We'll pick them up.

Of course, we'll have to take the seat out of the van to make room, but that can't be too hard to do. Let me check it out. Hmmm. The seat's bolted down. But, Bruce is strong. He'll be able to unbolt it. I wonder how much that bench seat weighs. And, it doesn't say anything in the manual about the seat being removable. But, if you take out the bolts, you can remove the seat. In my opinion, that makes it removable.

Moving along. If we set the fence posts eight feet apart, we'll need...hmm...oh, dear, that's quite a few. Might have to make more than one trip.

I called to order wire. "Oh? You don't deliver out here? Only in town?" Well, that's inconsiderate! "Okay, okay. We'll pick it up. Let's see. We need five rolls of one hundred feet. How big are they rolled up? Yikes! That big? Umm. I think we need to do...smaller. Let's make that ten rolls of fifty feet."

Oh, drat. That means we'll have to make more than one trip.

I asked, "How do you make concrete? You need what? Stones, concrete, sand, and water?" I don't think Bruce is going to like that recipe! "Don't you have some already made up? Like a cake mix or something?"

Oh, darn. Why isn't anything simple?

"Oh, you do have some that comes in bags and only needs water and sand? Good. We'll take it. How many bags will we need to do our project? That many? And, you say they're pretty heavy?"

We'll definitely have to make more than one trip.

"Hello? Sand company? I just need a small quantity of sand. You don't do small quantities? We have to buy how much? We don't need that much! Good grief, I just need a tad. Okay, okay. We'll take the minimum and let the kids have a sand pile with the rest. At least, you deliver.

"Lumberyard? How much do pickets cost? That much apiece! Good gracious, we need lots and lots. Let's see...that much, times lots and lots and lots. Oh, no! We can't afford that! I'll call you back."

Let me think. Is there any other way? I know! Let's check the JC Penneys catalog. Oh, no! Still way too expensive. What is it with you picket people? They're just boards.

Why so expensive? Can I do it another way? Oh, I know! I'll just buy boards, cut off the edges, and make my own spikie pickets!

Call the lumberyard. "Lumberyard? How much are six-foot-tall boards, picket width? Oh, great! Cheap."

Next problem. How do I cut off the edges and make a picket? Ask Dad. He knows lots about boards. Oh, good. He says I can borrow his electric saw to do the trimming. I can do this! I only have to make a few hundred pickets. How hard can that be?

Let's get to work on our fences!

We worked hard every evening and weekend. By the end of summer, our dog complex was complete. Bruce vowed he'd never put in another post, or attach any more wire, or pound any more staples, or dig any more holes, or make any more concrete. But, I could see the look of pride when he walked to our complex. And never is a long, long time.

I hired my teenage brother, Mark, to help me make pickets. I decided not to press my luck with Bruce. I wasn't sure about putting a saw in his hands after all the work my ideas had caused. I decided I didn't want to be known as the first headless woman in our area.

Mark and I spent hours making pickets by sawing off tips of boards, then pounding them onto boards I had attached to the posts Bruce had put in. That picket fence was the crowning touch. Now, it just needed to be painted. White. To match the house and buildings. Hmm. That means I need to paint the pasture fence white too. Think how awesome all that would be! Green grass and white fences. Just like in Kentucky.

Every day I did my chores, then gathered my paint and brushes. I was miffed because Bruce wasn't volunteering to help paint. His enthusiasm had waned. I tried to be understanding, but finally got really annoyed. I wanted to share the experience of painting our complex with him. I wanted to paint and chat. He wanted to watch baseball on television.

Okay, I admit on that Sunday I may have gotten a little mouthy. I suppose I shouldn't have assailed his manhood, lack of creative desire, and on and on.... He sneered at me and snapped, "Okay, okay!" He'd help paint the blasted fence if I would stop sulking and it would make me happy.

I didn't want him to do it to make me happy. I wanted him to do it because he wanted to do it. And, if he didn't want to do it...forget it! I didn't need help. I wanted companionship!

I stomped out to my fence and saw Bruce coming. I gathered all the brushes and hid them. I didn't need his stupid help!

He asked for a brush. I told him what he could do with any brush he could find and it was not paint the fence with it. He said I was acting childish. I told him to go to...Mars...and watch the ballgame! He demanded I give him a brush. I just kept painting with my three-inch brush and gave him the silent treatment. He said he really wanted to help.

It wasn't about helping. It was about...sharing quality time together. He just didn't understand, and I was definitely pouting by this time. The air was so frigid ice was forming.

He stood there thinking a few minutes, then stomped back into the house. I thought...blast you! No matter how much work you're doing on this place, I'm doing fifty times more!

I conveniently neglected to ponder on the fact that everything we were doing was my idea, not his. Therefore, perhaps it wasn't fair Bruce was spending his free time on my projects.

A few minutes later, Bruce was back. He had found a paintbrush. It had come from Sheri's paint set. Yes, indeed. A tiny, tiny brush used for painting pictures. I watched as he dipped the teeny brush into the paint bucket and proceeded to dab a drop or two of paint onto the fence. I figured, at that rate, he would still be painting thirty years later.

I tried to stay mad. His lips were set. He was, obviously, furious with me. But, there he was dabbing his little brush into the bucket, then smearing a drop or two onto the fence. I had to start laughing. How could I stay mad at anyone that determined to make a point? Generous Kathy gave him a four-inch brush, and we finished painting the pickets together. The next weekend we moved out to the pasture and worked our way around three acres.

You may be getting the idea that our lives were revolving around the needs of our show dogs. You would be correct. Special kennel, romping yard, grooming area, van, country living. All this to support a hobby that we loved.

As we settled into our kennel building and awesome romping yard, I realized we could use more storage area. I eyed the space above the inside kennels. It occurred to me that a shelf put on top of those kennels would give me 15´ x 5´ of storage space. Because the fencing was only five feet high, a shelf would be easily accessed. Think of all the stuff I could get up there!

I went to the lumberyard and explained what I wanted to do. I wanted to attach a wooden shelf to metal line pipes. They said there was no way to do that. I asked lots of questions. Isn't there something to use that will clamp onto the pipe on one end and nail to the boards on the other? Why can't I? There must be a way. Come on, you're guys. You must have a great guy idea!

They did have a "great guy idea." The guys told me to forget it.

I pouted all the way home. In my mind, I could see that shelf, full of my stuff, resting on the pipes. I studied the kennels, then came up with an idea. If I made a wood frame and sat it on top the kennel pipes, then attached sheets of pressed wood to the frame, the weight would keep the entire thing in place. It didn't need to be fastened. I ran my idea past Bruce. He was skeptical. He thought the thing would be too cumbersome and heavy to get up that high. I had to agree he was right. The building wasn't wide enough to make the shelf inside, then put it up that high.

Bruce told me to forget it and went off to the office. I studied the kennels, then had a brilliant idea! I could build the frame on top of the pipes by standing on a ladder. Then, I would slide pressed board sheets up onto the frame and nail the wood sheets to that frame.

The chain-link kennel fencing was nailed to studs through pressed board sheets that lined the inside of the building, so the fencing was very stable and secure.

I called Bruce and explained my terrific idea. I was excited. He told me to wait until he got home, and we would discuss it, because he didn't think it would work.

Oh phooey! There's the "wait" thing again! No way. I'm not waiting to listen to him try to talk me out of this super idea. I know! I'll do it and surprise him.

I went back to the lumberyard and bought studs and pressed board. I didn't tell them what I was going to do with my supplies because I didn't want a lecture on why it wouldn't work. I bought three, ½-inch thick 4´x6´ sheets of pressed board. That would make my shelf 6´x12´. With an adjustment of the frame size, it would fit perfectly. I was learning about measuring from Bruce.

Back at the kennel, I laid the studs across the pipes and nailed them together while dangling on the ladder. I was overcoming my fear of heights. Of course, I only had to stand on the first step, but, hey! High is high. Courage is courage.

Ouch! Blast! My thumb really hurts! How could I miss the nail and whack my thumb!

I hopped off the ladder, danced around in pain for a few minutes, then sucked it up and got back to work. I pounded and pounded and, finally...okay, the frame is done! Yea!!!!! You are so good, Kathy Boettcher, it only took an hour, and it's a perfect fit.

Hmm. A small glitch. I can get one sheet of pressed board up and onto the frame, but how to fasten it?

From the stepladder, I could only reach the front of the shelf. I couldn't get to the back of the shelf because of the building's wall.

I know! I'll climb up onto the sheet of pressed wood. My weight will hold it down while I pound nails and fasten the sheet to the frame. I'll just have to be careful not to stand on one side of the frame so it doesn't tip to the side and fall down.

Okay, up the ladder, kneel on the pressed board, carefully crawl across it...oh,drat! I forgot the nails!

Okay, back up slowly, find the stepladder with one foot, and... Ooowwww! Why did that dumb thing tip over? I hurt my knee! It's scraped. I might want to cry. Maybe this isn't such a great idea.

I looked around at my half-finished project, thought about Bruce's nasty remarks, wiped my tears of pain, set my mouth, stood up, slowly retrieved my hammer and nails, and put the stepladder back up.

Go up ladder, crawl across board, pound nail...whoa! This thing is wobbly! Take a deep breath! Don't move. Now, nail carefully. Oww. Oww. Oh, great, two more nail dings in my hand. Oh, who cares.

The work required a balancing act, slow movement, and a rather strange technique of pounding in nails. Getting down to put up the next sheet was tricky, but I managed without incident. Unless you count me dropping the hammer under the ladder, then standing up and smacking my head. I didn't count that because there was no blood or bump.

I was diligently pounding in the nails on my last sheet of pressed board when I heard his voice.

He said, "What do you think you're doing!"

Ooops. Busted. That sounds like Bruce. I'm not supposed to be doing this. I am definitely not supposed to be up here.

I took a page from my kid's book and answered. "Nothing."

He sighed and said, "Well, get your 'nothing' down here before you kill yourself!"

Excuse me? Kill myself? Where is the appreciation for the awesome talent that went into designing this shelf and the skill for bringing the project to a conclusion? Huh? Where is it?

I just kept pounding and sullenly finished while Bruce stood watching.

He helped me down, and I got lectured. But, I didn't care. I had a wonderful shelf. I had outsmarted the lumberyard guys. I had proven to Bruce my idea worked. And...nothing bad happened! (Unless you count all my boo-boos, which I didn't.) Hah on the universe and all men with no imagination!

The next day, I was cleaning inside of the five-foot-tall kennels. I forgot I had put the shelf in. I bent over, then stood straight up. Now, if you're under five-feet tall, this would not be a problem. But, when you're five-feet-seven inches tall? Let's just say the lesson left a lasting impression. I wobbled into the house and spent a couple hours on the sofa wondering if my brains had oozed into the bump on my head, or if said bump was only filled with the small amount of common sense I seemed to possess.

When Bruce came home and saw me lying there, he wanted to know what I had climbed up onto and fallen off of. Or what had I driven into?

I answered, haughtily, "Hah, on you! I didn't do any of that. I just stood up. I wasn't doing anything I shouldn't have!"

He sighed and shook his head. I could see doubt in his eyes.

About that time, there was a pounding on our door. The neighbor told us that Inky had been run over and was lying dead on the road. Oh, my goodness! A death!

The kids were sobbing. I was sniffling as we gathered Inky up for the funeral. She was a trifle flat, but I tried not to let the kids see that. We had a proper burial, said the eulogy and a prayer. It was so sad. When I told Mr. Farmer, he was not surprised. He said it happens all the time to country cats. Those words felt awful, but I knew he was right.

We waited the proper mourning interval and brought two more kittens named Pumpkin and Blue Eyes into our lives. Tiger tolerated the new additions, but didn't seem to be much into showing them the ropes.

A few days later, I was scooping poop in our large dog exercise yard. It was a beautiful day with white clouds lazing overhead. Brandie and Baku were romping, playfully, while I scrutinized the grass. Tiger was hunting in the backyard. I saw him leap up onto one of the fence posts and sit down. He was enjoying the sun. Brandie and Baku dashed over to visit the cat. I didn't think much about Tiger's perch being unsafe because the posts were six-feet high.

I was enjoying the day when I heard the most horrific yowl. It set the hair on the back of my neck right on end. My head swiveled in the direction of the sound. The fence post! Where was Tiger! Oh, no! He's in Brandie's mouth and Baku is trying to play tug-a-war with him.

"No! Stop that! He's not a tug-a-war! Let go!"

I started yelling at the dogs, ran to them, bopped Baku on the head with the pooper-scooper, dragged him into a kennel, and charged back to Brandie who was scampering away with her prey.

I grabbed Brandie's thick ruff and gave her a shake, all the time scolding and shouting. The cat, hissing and gasping, was firmly lodged in her mouth. I shook her again, sat her down, banged her with my hand, and tried to pry Tiger out of her mouth. I was rewarded for my efforts by the cat sinking his teeth into my hand. And, feline teeth are very, very sharp. Ooww! So much for gratitude, you ungrateful beast!

I managed to pry Brandie's mouth open and dislodge Tiger. Brandie immediately lunged for the cat, who was trying to climb up my arm. For a moment, I couldn't think what to do. Brandie was leaping at my hand. I used the other to keep her back, but she was strong. I glanced around for help. No one in sight. In that moment, I decided to toss Tiger over the fence. He might have a chance if he didn't splat too hard. If he stayed inside the yard, he had no chance at all.

I said a prayer and tossed Tiger up and over the fence. He landed, rolled over once, and didn't move.

Oh, no! Another cat death! And, I killed him!

Scolding Brandie at the top of my voice, using a few of my father's favorite nasty words, I dragged her into a kennel and raced for Tiger.

I cradled him in my arms. His eyes were dilated and he stared blankly at me. I yelled for the kids, grabbed a towel from the house, wrapped Tiger in it, herded everyone to the van, and drove to our vet. His office was in Waukesha, thirty minutes away. I prayed that Tiger wouldn't die before we got there.

When the receptionist saw Tiger's glazed eyes, she hustled us right in to a waiting room. Dr. Vet examined Tiger and said his gums were almost white from loss of blood. He took a large syringe and drew a full cylinder of blood from the cat's tummy. Dr. Vet took the cat in his arms and told us to go home. There was nothing they could do but monitor him.

Before I left the office, Dr. Vet took me aside, out of earshot of the kids and said he doubted Tiger would live through the night. I went home with an empty towel and a heavy heart.

The next morning, I took a deep breath and fearfully placed a call to the veterinary clinic. When I told the receptionist who I was, she asked when did I want to come after Tiger. I assumed she meant his body and asked, "When did he die?" She laughed and said he didn't die. He was just fine. Dr. Vet was amazed, but all Tiger's vital signs were normal and he could come home. It seemed Tiger put new meaning into the word "survivor."

Tiger was an outside cat who lived his life hunting. I tried to keep him indoors for a few days to make sure he recovered properly, but he was miserable. So, I decided it was time to let him out. He scampered to his little home in the shed, greeted Blue Eyes and Pumpkin, studied the exercise yard, then settled into his digs for a long nap. He never again went near the Siberian Huskies. That cat lived to be about fourteen years old. He survived many things over the years and used up more than nine lives. He moved to California with us, lived with another family for awhile, avoided coyotes in the canyons, came back to us, and moved back to Wisconsin with Sheri, where he took up residence in a farmer's barn.

When I remember Tiger, I am filled with warm, fuzzy feelings. He kept our yard free of gophers and mice, brought me gifts of dead critters, loved us all with friendly greetings of throaty purring, let us take him to the vet for checkups and shots, and never bit or scratched—except when Brandie was trying to eat him. I told Tiger I forgave him. If someone was trying to gobble me down, I might not be able to discern between friend and foe, either.

His favorite trick was to run toward you with a throaty greeting, then, as you approached, turn and walk away, only to flop directly in front of you. More than once I barely managed to avoid splishing his furry body into the ground as he just dropped over at my feet.

Several months later, Tiger developed a sore on his side. I took him to Dr. Vet, who examined the wound, then said to me, "Watch this."

I put my face close to the wound so I could observe. Dr. Vet pressed on both sides of the wound and out popped a grub. I almost threw up. That living, white, slimy, ugly, wiggly thing came out of my cat! Yuck-oh!

Dr. Vet laughed at the expression on my face, then explained something about flies, larva, flesh, and...I excused myself and went to the ladies room. Apparently, Dr. Vet thought it was amusing watching my face when the grub popped out and tried to crawl away. Idid not!

Frosty, in the meantime, was making friends with the milkman. However, I didn't know that's what the furry white beast was doing. When we first moved, we diligently tied Frosty up when he was let out in the morning to do his business. But, over the months, Frosty proved trustworthy and didn't stray from the property when he was left loose. We never left him outside, alone, for any length of time. The rule was, "Do your business, sniff and check the property, then get back inside." He conformed and at least some of our obedience training had reaped benefits.

One morning, I happened to glance outside shortly after Frosty had been let out for his morning constitutional. I saw him meander to the edge of our property, glance up the road, sit down and watch the milkman as he made deliveries at our two neighbors up the hill. Then, as the milk truck ambled down the road, Frosty stood and his tail started to wag. When the truck got even with our property, Frosty hurled himself into the open door, sat at the milkman's feet looking out, and rode into our driveway.

I could not believe my eyes. When the milkman came to the porch, I apologized. He laughed and said Frosty always waited for him and hopped in for a ride on delivery days. They were buddies, and he enjoyed the dog's company.

After the milkman left, I lectured Frosty. "You couldn't wait until the truck stopped to get on board? Are you insane! Are you trying to kill yourself? What if you miss and fall under the tires? What, then, young man! For that matter, you shouldn't be hopping in at all!"

Frosty wagged, grinned, and...ignored me. A month later, he added the UPS man to his taxi service. If a truck door was open, Frosty would leap in and accompany the driver to our door. He loved the rides and the drivers thought he was quite a character.

The next week, we were getting ready for a weekend at a dog show. Brandie, Natasha, and Baku were entered. We planned on taking the children and Frosty along. Plans had been made for a Siberian Husky Club get-together on the show grounds. I had groomed Brandie and Baku. I temporarily tied Brandie to one of the doghouses in the exercise yard (I have no idea why I did that.) and went into the house for a snack.

It was around 8:00 in the evening. As I gobbled my snack, I told Jason to go to the kennel and make sure the runs were clean. He ambled out. A few minutes later, I heard screaming. Lots of screaming.

Bruce and I ran to the yard. Jason was sobbing that he let Natasha out of her run so he could clean it. He didn't notice Brandie tied to the doghouse. Natasha had attacked Brandie. And, this fight was for keeps. It was what I came to call "a silent" fight. No growling. No threatening barks. Just bloodlust and business.

I felt terrible. The fight was my fault. I was the one who had not told Jason that Brandie was tied out. And, Jason was crying he was sorry. It is one of those times when a parent feels like a total failure.

Bruce and I frantically tried to separate the dogs, but by this time Brandie had a firm grip on Natasha's face. I screamed at Bruce to grab Natasha's tail and pull her backward. Brandie was chained to the doghouse, so my thinking was that if the dogs were stretched out, Brandie might lose her grip. In the meantime, I was cursing at Brandie and smacking her on the head.

Bruce pulled Natasha back as far as he could, but Brandie was not about to let go. Bruce reached for Brandie's face, thinking if he smacked her nose, she might let go. In that moment, Brandie lost her grip and Natasha retaliated. Unfortunately, Natasha didn't get Brandie. She got Bruce's hand. Sort of like the way Tiger had nailed me. However, my bite was small. Bruce's hand was in Natasha's mouth.

But, an amazing thing happened. When Natasha felt his hand, she let go. I dragged her into the kennel and shakily checked Bruce's hand. Even though Natasha hadn't bitten down the way she could have, she had caught two of his fingers. There was a small tooth mark on the outside edge of each finger. It looked small to me, but they were bleeding. Because I wasn't sure what shots Bruce had as a child or what might be needed, I decided a trip to the emergency room was in order.

While I was wrapping his hand, I told Sheri to go get Natasha and clean her up. After all, we were leaving for the dog show early in the morning.

Before I could get Bruce ready to leave, Sheri was back telling me Natasha was hurt. I gave my shaking husband an aspirin and raced to the kennel. Natasha was sitting on the grooming table. I remember thinking, she's not hurt. Thank goodness.

I checked her face. Oh, no! Natasha had a slash mark across the top of her eye. It was a couple inches long and I could see bone. Let me tell you, bone is not something you want to see on the face of your show dog. Or any other dog for that matter.

I also noticed her nose was not attached to her face in quite the same manner as it had been. Blood dripped from both wounds.

Okay, I have two victims. Both are bleeding. One's fingers are wrapped and he's been given aspirin as a painkiller. The other victim is oozing blood.

Triage became something I got quite good at over the years. I crated Natasha in the van, escorted Bruce to the passenger seat, loaded the kids in back, and drove...straight to the vet who I had called. Dr. Vet was not pleased to have a patient at that time of night on a Friday. He had gone home and had to come back to the clinic. But, he did consider Natasha's wounds an emergency.

Bruce muttered something about why did the dog come first? I explained she was a show dog and he was only a mere stud. He was not amused.

Dr. Vet examined Natasha and said he would have to shave her face, stitch her back together, and we could take her home.

I paled. Shave? My show dog! Surely you jest!

Now, everyone involved in the sport of dogs will understand my horror. To those of you who are logical and say, "Well, of course you have to shave the face to stitch," let me explain something. Sometimes, when dogs are shaved, the hair doesn't come back in quite the same way. And, when you're showing dogs, this trivial stuff is not TRIVIAL!

I gasped, then said, "Can't you do it without shaving her face?"

It was Dr. Vet's turn to pale. He answered, "Well, I can, but that makes it very hard!"

I smiled and said, "Let's go for hard. She's beautiful and I want to keep her that way."

He glared at me, but took Natasha into the back for her stitches. Dr. Vet muttered something about, "Ridiculous show dog people!"

He did an outstanding job. You couldn't see the stitches woven in between black and white dog hairs. And, unless you stared at Natasha's nose, you wouldn't notice that it had been reattached to her face. Dr. Vet assured me that it was okay to show Natasha the next day. She seemed unaffected by her boo-boo.

However, one week later, Dr. Vet's partner, who was the one available to take out the stitches, was not a happy camper. It seems the stitches were so well hidden, he couldn't find them to remove. After thirty minutes of perspiring, he finally located the last one and left, grumbling about a meeting with Dr. Vet and a conference about stitches, and the next time Dr. Vet put them in that way, he could darn well take them out himself!!

On the evening of the accident, after putting Natasha in her crate, I drove to the hospital and took Bruce into the emergency room. He didn't need stitches, only a couple of shots.

On our way home, I smugly told him I had put my patients in the proper order. He snapped something about being the breadwinner and in charge and, therefore, the most important. Hmmm. He does have a point. Oh, well. Maybe next time.

He grumbled, "There better not be a next time!"

Interestingly enough, even though Brandie appeared to be the victor in the confrontation, the balance of power had shifted. Natasha carried herself differently. It was a blend of swagger and "get out of my face."

From that day forward, Natasha was top dog. She was top dog until the day she died. Whenever Natasha ran free in our yard, any Siberian who ran with her ran just behind her shoulder, never in front, and that included our males. If Natasha was let out of her kennel, she always ran directly to Brandie and growled threateningly. It was an obvious challenge that Brandie did not back away from. She would leap at the fence with teeth bared. We never again let them run together. They were fine together on leashes or on the sled with us, but we all knew running free together was not going to work until one of them forced the other to belly up. And, neither one was going to give in if there was a breath of life in them. I wanted a breath of life in both of them, so I decided they were never going to be "chums" and I was going to have to accept that.

Actually, there are some people who I never want to be chums with too. So, I respected Brandie and Natasha's dislike for each other. That is, as long as it didn't involve blood, guts, and other things.

Natasha had become "leader of the pack."

A few weeks later, we were off to another show. It was an exciting event because we were staying at a motel that catered to dog show participants. We were staying in a group of rooms rented by the Siberian Husky club members. Our van was loaded to the hilt with four dog crates, grooming table and equipment, luggage, dog food and supplies, plus various other indispensable items like kids and a husband.

Bruce backed the van into a parking spot just in front of our motel room. The guys were standing around chatting while the gals checked out the rooms. Our van's back doors were open as was the sliding side door. I was impatient to unload. Bruce ignored my glares. I was always impatient about everything, and he was used to ignoring me.

I climbed into the passenger seat to get something out of the glove compartment. I had my sunglasses in one hand. I accidentally dropped them onto the driver's floor mat. When I reached to get them, they slid under the seat.

I sighed disgustedly. I thought about going around the van and opening the driver's door to get at the glasses, but a friend had pulled very close to us and the driver's door barely opened.

I thought a moment, then decided to access the driver's area by coming into the van through the side door. We had all kinds of stuff sitting on the bench seat and floor. I wiggled across the pile, across the large box-like area that housed shifting apparatus, rested on the stuff with my belly, and reached for the glasses. I couldn't reach them. I stretched out. Still couldn't reach them. I stretched further, got a finger on them, managed to take hold, and tried to back up.

Uh-oh. I seem to be stuck.

I had tipped so far forward, I couldn't get back. I was stuck on my tummy with my fanny and legs in the air. I wiggled. I tried everything. Nope. Stuck.

I could hear Bruce and Pete talking behind the van.

I thought, I could call Bruce. Oh, rats! If he has to help me, I'll never, ever hear the end of it! There has to be a way out of here.

I struggled and, in the end, just sighed. It was no use, I was stuck.

I called out softly, "Bruce."

I didn't want anyone else to see me.

No response. I tried calling, softly, again. Nothing but masculine chuckles and joke telling going on.

Blast it! Here I am, stuck for life, and those guys are just passing time!

Finally, I bellowed, "BRUCE!"

I heard the voices stop.

Bruce said, "Kathy? Where are you?"

"Ummm. In here."

A moment later, Bruce was at the side door. I said, "Bruce, just grab my leg and pull me out. Don't tell anyone, okay?"

There was silence, then I heard him start to laugh. The next thing I know, he's calling for Pete. "Hey, Pete! Look at this! I need help!" Bruce chortled.

Those idiot guys stood there, laughing, while the blood rushed to my head. So much for sympathy.

As they chortled as only men can, each one grabbed an ankle and dragged me out. It took several months for me to live that one down.

We spent the summer and autumn working on the property and showing dogs. It was a time of learning and experiencing. The farmers in the area put up with all my stupid questions and antics. I would wander into the local feed store, check to see what was going on locally, and chat. I loved it.

I joined the PTA and volunteered to help children with reading difficulties. So, a couple days each week, I went to Jason's small country school and spent an hour trying to convince an incorrigible six-year-old girl that reading was important and she really could learn to do it. That is...if she would just sit still and look at the book.

"Please sit down and let's read! It's fun! It's...no, no. Come back here! Running around the room isn't the best approach even if you are carrying the book. It's hard to read the book if it's tucked under your arm. You can't see the words that way.

"I know you like to play the piano sitting over there, but...how about this. You read a page and you can plunk three notes. You read another page and you can plunk five notes. How about we deal here, kid? Work with me."

I admit my approach was probably unorthodox. However, the negotiation paid off. We plunked. We read. And, she improved.

I guess my approach to life, in general, has been a trifle unconventional. But, oh, well. I tried. I hope that counts for something when I go back to wherever I came from. There are those that think I came from hell, but I think that's a trifle harsh.

Chapter Five

I was about to get a lesson in what not to do when your female is in season. Now, the proper term for a female dog is bitch. I shuoldn't use that term in this book because there are those who are offended by it, but I for one, am not.

Natasha came into season. That's the cycle where a female can be bred. I knew Natasha was coming into season because she was flirting with Baku, Bruce, Tiger, the fence post, and anything else that stood still. But, I was naïve. I had read that the breeding time was that magic 10–14 days within the season of 21 days. So, I assumed she could not conceive at any other time.

Wrong.

I had no plans to breed at that time. We had no room for a litter, and I had way too much going on. It seems Natasha and Baku had other plans. They decided it was time to start a family.

Sheri was cleaning the kennel. I told her it was okay to let Baku and Natasha run together. I take full responsibility for what happened next. It went like this:

First, I hear Sheri shrieking.

I'm thinking, Dog fight! Dog fight! Dead cat! Captured mole!

I run to the kennel and see Natasha and Baku

doing...what? Oh, my goodness! Get them apart! They can't do that outside in broad daylight!

I raced to the phone and called Baku's co-owner Mae. I babbled that they were stuck together. She said congratulations, the babies would be due in about sixty days.

Babies! Good grief! I don't want babies! I...

I endured her lecture about keeping females away from males the entire time they are in season. She was not pleased that Baku had sired a litter. As if I was! He had not yet been x-rayed and certified with the Orthopedic Foundation for Animals that he did not have hip dysplasia. Many dog breeds are afflicted with hip dysplasia which, in simple terms, means the upper thigh bone does not properly fit into the hip socket. It can be a painful condition and you do not want to breed dogs that have it, as it can be passed to offspring. At that time, dogs had to be two years old before they could be x-rayed and registered.

Natasha was just short of being two years by a few months. It was important to all Siberian Club members that breeding stock be certified clear of hip dysplasia and eye disorders.

Oh, goodness! I'm a failure! Again!

I lectured Baku when he finished dating Natasha. He ignored me. Baku was definitely one happy guy.

A few days later, I took them both to Dr. Vet and explained my hip dysplasia dilemma. He palpated both dogs' hips and said he thought their hips were fine. Later, they both were x-rayed and certified with perfect hips. But, I must admit, I worried while waiting for x-ray proof.

In those moments, I had become a "dog breeder." And, in the future, would become a breeder who loved every dog we ever bred or bought with all my heart and spirit. They brought indescribable joy into my life.

Sixty days later, the first litter was born. I insisted we build a whelping box, for mom and pups, and keep it in the kitchen. We held Natasha's paw through her labor and were rewarded with five adorable puppies—three females and two males. I had hoped Natasha would not pass her coat break to her offspring. But, one male had a small white spot, the other a huge white shoulder. One female had a small white shawl, the other a large white shoulder, and the third a white spot.

As the weeks passed, the kitchen became a staging area for puppies and their antics. There was always a puppy underfoot. I saw them take their first wobbling steps. I enjoyed puppy breath while they licked my chin. They would sit across from each other, growl and grumble, then try to bite their siblings. They would latch on to each other's noses and growl fiercely. Challenging each other, and trying to establish a pecking order begins very early. They learned to climb out of the whelping box and explore the kitchen. When they began eating their first solid food, it was just like a human baby's experience. Mushed food was all over their faces and the floor. They became coordinated enough to chase balls and chew on...everything! We all enjoyed every moment and even the cleaning up was acceptable.

When I was alone with my brood, I would put rock music on and dance around the kitchen with a puppy in my arms. Their ears would flop up and down with the music. They loved dancing with me. I would gyrate around the kitchen and the other four puppies would be pawing at my legs for their turn. I'd plop my partner down, grab another, and away we'd go. I could feel their happiness at being included. We definitely had chorus line potential.

When they reached six weeks, they were just too much for our kitchen, and it was time to move them into the kennel.

Actually, it was time to sell them. But, how can I part with my dance partners? I've gotten attached. They're like my little kids.

"Bruce, can't we at least keep one? Just one?"

"Okay."

"But, Bruce, I can't decide which one. How about we keep one male and one female?"

"Okay. I suppose that's all right."

"Bruce, I can't let strangers take my little guys and gals. I know! We'll keep the two best females, and the two males. We'll sell the one with the longer coat. How's that for a compromise?"

"Compromise! Is that what you call it? That means we'll have seven Siberian Huskies. Have you lost your mind?"

I batted my eyes at him and said, "You'd have a team for sledding. You know Natasha doesn't like to run on the sled. We can train the little guys and gals. Then, you can be a real musher with a big team." (I hoped this ploy would work. All guys want the biggest...whatever.)

He caved.

We sold the long-coated female to a great family. I admit I cried when she left.

We put four free-standing chain-link kennels on the concrete slab between the garage and kennel building. Fastening four kennel runs together gave them the stability that one did not have. Then, I set about training my new guys and gals. We named them Bruka's Kojak of Catca, Bruka's Apuka of Catca, Bruka's Tabu of Catca, and Bruka's Tanta of Catca. I added the "Catca" because I thought it sounded cool. It had no meaning and I should not have put it in the names. People often thought it was another kennel. Nope. Just Kathy playing mind games.

So, now we were hauling puppies to conformation classes. Every week the gang went with Sheri and me for training. The puppies had awesome personalities. Apuka turned out to be one of my favorites. He did some winning as a puppy, but didn't have the look judges favored. Apuka was a tad tall, his coat was a smidge bushy, and he was mismarked with a huge white shoulder. But, he was the most wonderful, kind, gentle, loyal dog I have ever owned. Eventually, I used him on my two-dog sled team. And, when I crashed that sled into a tree and knocked myself unconscious, I woke up to him gently licking my face. My last memory, after smacking that tree, was seeing the sled careening behind Apuka and Tanta as they sped down the trail around a curve. Fear welled in me, and I thought they were gone forever.

I passed out. When I woke to that gentle kiss, I realized Apuka was still harnessed to both Tanta and the sled. She was laying in the snow, resting. He was trying to rouse me. Someplace, down the trail, he realized I wasn't with them, turned the sled back, and found me. I still tear up with loving emotion when I think about him.

He came close to death when he was one year of age, but survived even after Dr. Vet gave up on him. Apuka should have died in those moments. I nursed him and watched his eyes glaze with pain and his coat fall out. He lost weight, and just when I thought all was lost, he suddenly did a turnaround.

I cannot describe the joy I felt when the light came back on in Apuka's dark brown eyes. He had courage, loyalty, and a loving personality.

How do you measure the size of a friend's heart? You put it next to Apuka's.

My friend, Apuka, did have one bad habit. His favorite game was to start toward me at a dead run, gather speed, leap for my chest, and kiss my chin. Somehow, he managed to curtail his speed at the last moment, so there was hardly any impact. I loved this game and would laugh as he slurped my face. He stopped doing it a few years later when we had a large kennel that was being taken care of while we were off on a show circuit. It seems Apuka tried to play the "kiss, kiss" game with the kennel sitter, who raised Alaskan Malamutes, and the guy decked Apuka with a pooper-scooper. Our kennel sitter's experience with his Alaskan Malamutes was, if they were jumping for your face and throat, you better defend yourself. He apologized for knocking Apuka on his butt and said he only wobbled for a little while. He cured Apuka of jumping and doing "kiss,

kiss." And, in retrospect, it was probably a good thing. I could see how that behavior might have been taken as a threatening move or, in the least, as a better brace yourself or I'll knock you over.

Kojak was a winner from the get-go. He was perfectly balanced and outgoing. He won numerous puppy awards and easily finished his championship. Kojak became our lead dog on Bruce's sled team the winter that he raced. Remember me mentioning that I loved to take one of my Siberians, tie him to a bicycle, and careen along forest trails? My cohort in crime was Kojak. We spent hours in the forest, bumping along winding paths.

He loved running and was extremely intelligent. One time, when Bruce was racing across a lake, the course was changed due to bad weather. Snow was blowing and obliterating the marked trail. The race officials began turning teams around. Bruce said Kojak was upset because they wouldn't allow him to take the trail. He knew where he was supposed to go and wanted to go that way. But, he listened to orders and turned around. My champion had brains as well as brawn.

Let me explain how important dog names become to dog breeders. We ponder. We fret. We want the perfect name. We want a name that reflects certain things—strength, intelligence, heritage, personality. Apuka, Tabu, and Tanta all had special meanings. Then, how did we come up with Kojak? It goes like this. I wanted to include the family in the naming process and was taking suggestions. Jason wanted the name Kojak because he loved the TV show. My knee-jerk reaction to Jason's suggestion was...no way! But, I could see how much it meant to Jason to name the puppy. So, I gave in. Of course, that dog became our biggest winner up to that point in time. Kojak. Of all the names in the universe that conjure up sledding, Kojak was not one of them.

So, you see, naming strategy can go astray. In our case, it happened more than once.

Years later, there was the male who Bruce named. Bruce wanted to call him Bruka's Sentinal Haznosput. Let me explain the haz...no...sput. The dog was not mismarked in any way. No coat break. He did not have a white shoulder or spot. Get it? Haz...no...spot. Bruce didn't want the meaning to be obvious so it became Haznosput. You cannot believe how many times I had to explain that ridiculous name. The dog became Sputty to the family. And...you guessed it. He became our biggest winner. Sputty obtained his championship with ease and went on to compete against other champions. He placed several times in the Working Group and, eventually, became a group winner. He also became the number seventeenth ranked Siberian Husky male in the United States one year. American Canadian Champion Bruka's Sentinal Haznosput. Egad. Think of all the wonderful monikers that one could have had. It boggles the mind.

Okay, so where are we? Oh, yes. Seven Siberian Huskies and one Westie. Hmm. Only one Westie? He sleeps with Sheri, so Jason feels left out. I know! Let's get Jason a Westie female. Maybe I do want to show Westies. And, this time I'll do it right. I'll go to a breeder.

That's exactly what I did and we acquired Marantha's Miss Betwitchin'. Pixie for short. Pixie was a darling. She also had a mouth that wouldn't quit. She cried for days after we brought her home. It broke my heart. So, I solved the problem by putting her crate right next to our bed. She'd cry and whimper. I'd put a finger through the crate and touch her. This continued, off and on, all night long. I did this for years. Okay, maybe it only seemed like years. It might have been weeks. I was determined that she would sleep in her crate.

Of course, Frosty, by now, was sleeping on Sheri's bed even though Mom wanted him in his crate at night.

Imagine my surprise when one night I went in to check on Sheri and reached to tuck her in. A sleeping Frosty thought I was an intruder, woke from a sound sleep nestled under her covers, and grabbed my hand.

I was so shocked I did what anyone would do. I reacted by shaking my hand and cursing. Unfortunately, Frosty lost his grip and went sailing off the bed crashing into the wall. He only wobbled around dazed for a few minutes. I was furious at first, then realized he was protecting Sheri. My hand was bruised, not bitten. Frosty let go when he realized he had nabbed the hand that fed him. I decided him sleeping with Sheri was a good idea because Frosty's priority was protecting her. True, Frosty was small, but he had attacked a looming figure in the dark. I was proud of him. I knew that he would protect Sheri no matter what it cost him. How many of us have loyal friends like that?

Jason was whining that it wasn't fair Frosty could sleep with Sheri, but Pixie had to be crated in our bedroom. I explained Pixie was a puppy and might do nasty things in his bed. He thought a moment and decided this was one of the very few times Mom might be right. But, he wanted Pixie in his room at night. I gladly relinquished my charge to Jason. I think he lived to regret that decision, but wasn't about to admit Mom might have been right. I'm not sure how many weeks it took before Pixie gave up her nightly crying. And...of course...eventually, she joined Jason in bed.

Cold winter days gave way to the sun warming, earth turning green, trees budding, and birds returning from the south. Weeks were filled with chores, kids, and dog shows. Life was good.

As summer approached, the entry form arrived for the Waukesha Kennel Club show. I studied it and saw they were featuring a "team" class. As I read the requirements, I thought, my guys and gals look alike. I have a team! Maybe I could do this.

The requirements were: Four dogs would be shown at the same time. They had to look alike. They would go through the routine as a unit with one handler. That included gaiting for the judge and standing for examination. Practically speaking, that meant I would have four dogs to my left on one leash. The four of them would be required to stand still while the judge went over each one. We would gait up and back for the judge, stand with expression, then gait around the ring. Each dog had to be entered in an individual class in order to qualify for the team class.

I thought, This is intriguing. The puppies will be six months old by show time and can be entered in the regular classes. They've all been shown many times at fun matches and know the routine. They're well trained and handle easily. How hard can it be to simply hook them together and do it as a team? Not that hard. There's that ridiculous, optimistic, naïve streak showing through again.

I remember the conversation with Bruce. Up to this time, I was merely considering the possibility. When I told him about the team class and suggested my puppies, he started to chuckle. He looked me in the eye and his chuckles turned to laughter, complete with tears of amusement. It seems to me he chortled something about, "You have got to be kidding! That's the funniest thing I've ever heard. You'll never be able to control all four of them at one time." Or, words to that effect.

My eyes narrowed. The man had just thrown down the gauntlet, and I never walk away from a gauntlet. I picked it up and sneered, "You just watch me, buster!"

He sobered and looked shocked. "You are not, actually, going to try this, are you?"

I said, indignantly, "I am not going to try it! I'm going to do it!"

I was livid. How dare he laugh at me! I was training dogs almost every day. And, by this time, we were going to shows several times a month. I knew my stuff! Or, at least, I thought I did.

I entered the show. I put Kojak in a bred-by-exhibitor class and Apuka in a puppy class. I entered Tabu in the bred-by-exhibitor class and Tanta in a puppy class. I entered the boys in a brace class. I entered the girls in the bitch brace class. Then, I entered them as a team. The requirements for the brace class were the same as the team class except it was done with two dogs.

Looking back, I may just have stepped into the true definition of lunacy or, perhaps the twilight zone. But, I was determined to make a point. I'm no longer sure, exactly, what that point was, but....

Bruce just shook his head and kept giggling. Every day, with a gleam in his eye and a smile on his lips, he asked me how I was doing. I hemmed and hawed and kept putting off training day. I naïvely thought it wouldn't take very much to put the guys and gals together and be a "show team." After all, they were superbly trained as individuals.

When I'm wrong...I'm really wrong.

A few weeks before the big day, I decided I better give it all a try. I hooked my four together and disaster struck. It was quite apparent that working as individuals did not qualify for working together.

I thought, This can't be happening! These are Siberian Huskies. Working as a team must be inbred! Why are we tangled up? Why are they quarreling with each other? Why are they wound around me?

After an exhausting hour, I knew I was in deep doodoo. I had spent a small fortune on entry fees. Word had gotten around that I was showing a team. And...and Bruce was just waiting for me to fall on my face. In this case, that was going to be literally.

As I sat on the front stoop, contemplating and visualizing my humiliation, Sheri plopped down beside me. She asked, "You got troubles, Mom?"

If Bruce had asked the same thing, I would have denied it. Instead, I nodded and sighed, "Oh, yes."

Sheri thought a moment, then offered to help. At first, I dismissed her suggestion as a child just wanting to help Mom. But, she stubbornly repeated it. She thought, instead of working them as a team, I needed to start over and work one at a time. Then, add one and do a brace of two. Once they were comfortable with being a brace, we could put them together as a foursome. She would work the girls. I could work the boys. Then, she would help, when I put the team together, by following us and making corrections if the dog's misbehaved. Even at that age, Sheri had the makings of a fine trainer. Her Mom, on the other hand, was...I'm truly not sure what I was.

I thought, That's an incredibly good idea!

I started over. I could tell you that it was easy and worked the first time. However, I'm going to confess. It went something like this:

1. My gals and guys thought the idea of being hooked together for the brace and team was a fun, silly game. So, they played. With each other. With me. Problem? Game playing involves batting each other with paws, batting Mom, bumping, and playing ring around the rosy—I mean ring around the Mom.

2. I tried initially to use four individual show leads wrapped in my left hand. This can be a problem. Why, you ask? Because they tangle when the dogs are playing. Or, they go in different directions when the Siberians decide this exercise makes no sense. Or, they wind around your legs and you fall. And, because there's too much slack, this approach leads to small, but very intense, arguments between said guys and gals which require loud, nasty vocalization on the part of the handler, and guardian angels' raised, disapproving eyebrows.

3. I switched to choke chains and brace couplers. This was good. This gives better control. Now, we have control, but we have two braces going in separate directions. Why, oh, why do the guys not want to go in the same direction as the gals? Okay, now we've got them going in the same

direction. However, it is not the direction in which I am going.

4. Okay, now we've reached agreement, and they understand where Mom goes, they go. That's all well and good if we're going in a straight line. However, in the show ring we have to make a circle, a triangle, and, heaven forbid, the dreaded "L" pattern. As we tried to learn these patterns, we regressed to trip, fall, shove, and loud nasty vocalization on the part of the handler.

5. At this point, I decided I needed a lead dog. A pack leader. A subordinate who adored Mom and would force the pack to do the same. That would be Apuka, who dearly loved me, and almost always did what I said. I put him right next to me, so he could show the others what needed to be done. He had to literally push the team away at the corners. This may not sound difficult, however, you must understand how hard it is to shove three revved up Siberians in any direction. Apuka proved he could always be counted on to take direction from me and enforce my edicts. Well, maybe not *always*. If he thought I was scolding too much, he pouted and lagged. Badly. I called it a Fat Puka snit. (Because his coat was longer, Apuka always looked slightly disheveled and I dubbed him "Fat Puka.") The challenge was trying to get a lagging Fat Puka up to me when the dogs he was connected to were forging ahead. If he got frustrated, he would just sit down, fouling up everyone. This caused tangles like you cannot imagine. Solution? You must be nice to Fat Puka, always telling him how wonderful he is and, at the same time, scream at the other three.

Tabu was my outside female. She was sensitive. If I corrected her more than once, she would put her ears down and drop a mile back. Guess what? Now, I had the inside dog and the outside dog lagging with hurt feelings, and the two middle clowns, who let nothing in the world deter them from a good time, leaping ahead. Why am I doing this! Tears look so ridiculous on a grown, middle-aged woman!

6. After two weeks of practicing every day, I had everybody in a good mood and all working well together. That is until our cat went for a stroll in front of us. Question: How can four dogs, hooked together at the neck, still chase a cat up a tree? I appreciated Sheri not telling her Dad that I was crying and babbling, incoherently, after saving the cat and spending thirty minutes trying to untangle everyone while threatening to give up dog training forever. I also appreciated her not busting me to her grandmother and father for my use of foul language. Very, very foul language.

We have some old photos that Sheri took of our training sessions. They are of dogs tangled around my legs. Dogs chasing a cat. Dogs mouthing each other as they gaited. Dogs standing, one facing front and one facing rear. Dogs wound up with each other. Dogs jumping in my face and vying for the title of best face licker.

However, Sheri and I worked every single day and, by show time, we were ready. Sort of. I was a nervous wreck. But, my team did know what was expected of them.

As we stood outside the ring, I wondered whatever had possessed me. People were watching and waiting...probably for disaster to strike. Rumor had it that the last team shown had ended up in a terrible fight, complete with blood, that took several people to break up.

Sheri's and my work paid off. The guys and gals handled beautifully. We went on to show as a team in the group and best of show classes. We took Best Team in Show. Of course, we were the only team in the show, but who cared? We did it!

I showed the team for over a year at shows in various states and we even flew the team to California for a national specialty. Each time, they made me proud. Each time, I was flirting with disaster, but didn't know it. Sometimes, it's better not to realize what can happen.

One summer day, I was waiting to go into the Best in Show ring with the team. A well-known handler came up to me and said he was very impressed with my team. He had watched them in the breed and group rings. He wanted to know if I was worried that they would fight.

I smiled, smugly, and said, "My team would never fight. Not ever." I thought, They argue occasionally, but I have perfect control.

Why had I not learned about tempting fate? What is wrong with my feeble brain?

I confidently gaited my team into the ring. It was huge, and we were passing in front of a row of judges. I was using the two brace couplers—one for the guys and one for the gals. I always ran with the boys close to me because they were bigger than the girls and it looked better that way. What I didn't know was that my young ladies were coming into season. And that my boys were becoming men.

As we gaited, I heard the grumbling, then growling. My boys had decided to fight over the girls. Apparently, sex was on their minds instead of impressing judges. My life passed before me. Picture four dogs fighting to the death in front of a row of judges.

Bumping was added to the growling. I spoke sharply under my breath, "Knock it off!"

They stopped quarreling, but as we rounded the turn and came back, the bumping took on epic proportions, and the growling started again. I did what any red-blooded musher does under those circumstances. Remembering my manners, I smiled at the judges as I passed. I always held the leashes in my left hand which left my right hand free. As I smiled, I banged each dog on top the head with my right fist and kept on going. As I left the ring, I waited for the reprimand. You are not allowed to discipline dogs in the ring.

Apparently, no one noticed or, perhaps, they were just being discreet knowing what could have happened if I hadn't nipped the brawl in the bud. When I asked Bruce, he said you couldn't tell what I was doing or that the dogs were misbehaving. Heaven smiled on me that day.

It smiled on me twice that day. I met a woman who would become my cohort and friend. She loved the team and came over to compliment me. It turned out she lived just down the road from us. She had Doberman Pinschers and Norwich Terriers. We became instant friends. Her name was Lea. As she chatted, we discovered we liked all the same things and adventures. Imagine the luck of meeting a woman with my life philosophy. And, she lived just down the road! I was thrilled. Bruce paled. So did Lea's husband.

Everything was going great. The house, yard, fences, and outbuildings looked wonderful. I had given up gardening but kept the yard and pasture mowed. The property was green, lush, and well cared for. My kids were thriving in the country. They rarely complained about all the chores, and I was proud of them. Also, I was happy with myself for recognizing that keeping our kids busy kept them out of trouble. Our dogs were well trained and winning. We were traveling to dog shows and having fun. We had one of the few teams in the country and received accolades for that accomplishment. I was attending dog classes, making lots of friends, and loved all my dogs and doggie duties.

Why, oh, why, did I not leave well enough alone? What is wrong with me? What is there about well-ordered routine that drives me to do strange things?

Chapter Six

As summer blossomed, Lea and I became close friends. Lea, her husband, and two sons had rented an old farm down the road from us. It had been a dairy operation for decades and had an immense barn, outbuildings, picket-fenced yard, and the most incredible turn-of-the-century farmhouse. The dairy operation had shut down, and all animals were sold. Lea and I would hurry through our individual chores, then I would go to her place. We spent hours exploring the old buildings and talking about dog training, breeding, and care. The old dairy farm was awesome.

Once in a while, I'd buy a dozen doughnuts, and we would sit talking in her kitchen, drinking coffee and stuffing our faces. We ate doughnuts for breakfast, lunch, and snack time. Once we went into Waukesha to buy doughnuts at a local bakery, and it started to pour rain. I moaned about getting wet.

She laughed and said, "Let's walk in the rain!"

I was aghast. Get wet? Why?

But, Lea was out the door. I reluctantly followed. We spent an hour walking in warm rain, laughing, window shopping, munching doughnuts, and enjoying the moment. I haven't walked in the rain, just for fun, since, but I have never forgotten those moments of freedom.

I told Lea how much I loved to ride horses. I drooled over her quarter horse. I had spent a few years in my early thirties learning to ride hunt seat. I did some beginner jumping. Before getting involved with dogs, I rode at least once a week. I had always wanted my own horse. Now, we had the pasture and the room.

Lea had a friend who was selling a mare. We went to the stable where Babe was being kept, and I fell in love with the brown mare. Of course, I had never bought a horse before. I didn't know the pitfalls and, believe me, there are many. I was far too trusting, but my guardian angels were watching out for me.

I could see myself galloping across the fields every day. My horses had always been ready for me to ride. I had done no research in the proper care of horses. I didn't understand what really goes into taking care of one. I was an idiot. A well-intentioned idiot, but an idiot, nonetheless. Babe was everything the owner said. She was healthy and well trained. There was a small glitch, however. One I would discover a few weeks later. Babe didn't like to turn left. Ever try to gallop across the fields and never turn left? It makes it hard to get home.

I pleaded with Bruce. Could I buy Babe? She wasn't that expensive. You would think I would have learned about costs by having the dogs. Remember Brandie? She was free. Perhaps I should have tallied up what we had spent since obtaining her. However, that thought never occurred to me.

Of course, buying Babe meant we would have to add a small barn to our kennel. She could be pastured in summer, but not in winter. As it turned out, one of our dog friends had a brother-in-law who was a construction person. We contacted him, discussed plans for a small barn, got an estimate, sat down, and decided we could afford Babe.

I was ecstatic! Not only was I getting the horse I had always dreamed about, I was getting a barn too. I carefully designed the new addition and decided to put in two stalls just in case we acquired another horse in the future. The barn was tiny with the two 12'x12' stalls, a storage space, and an aisle. Both stalls opened into the pasture with double Dutch doors. Of course, we would need a small corral to keep the horses contained when we didn't want them in the entire pasture. And, that meant...you guessed it...more fencing.

Poor Bruce. He just groaned, even though I assured him it would only be a small area. He grumbled something about define...small. I laughed and said smaller than the three-acre pasture. He was not amused.

Lea agreed to keep Babe at her place until the barn was completed. We arranged to have a man trailer my beautiful mare over to Lea's. Then, I bought a saddle, saddle blanket, bridle, halter, lead rope, grain, and grooming supplies. Guess what? My cheap horse wasn't as cheap as I thought. Factor in the new fence and barn and, hmmm. Is nothing cheap?

Lea and I rode every chance we got. It was wonderful. We galloped across fields just like in my daydream. I discovered Lea's idea of fun was to race. Babe loved to gallop, but she was much slower than Lea's palomino. I learned something I want to share with you. You know those cowboy movies where the posse is galloping along the trail chasing after the crook? Want to know why they compete for the lead spot? Macho toughness? Prestige? Enthusiasm? Nope. The guys behind the leader eat a great deal of dirt. I had never realized how much dirt a galloping horse churns up until I ate it. After every race, I was filthy!

I trained dogs, took care of my small house, mowed grass, went to dog shows, rode my horse, visited with Lea, did summer fun things with the kids, and enjoyed life to the fullest.

The phone rang late one summer afternoon. It was Lea, panic in her voice. Our horses had escaped and were galloping down the highway. I don't have to tell you how dangerous that was for the horses and anyone not expecting a horse to be racing toward their car.

I said I'd be right there. I hung up the phone, told the kids to stay put, ran to the van, and drove to Lea's. Before I could get out of the van, she was steaming toward me. She said a neighbor had called, and the horses were trotting around their yard. Lea carried two bridles. She jumped into the van, and we drove a mile down the road.

Sure enough, Babe and the palomino were trotting up and down the driveway, around the house, and eluding the farmer who was trying to catch them. He glared at us. Lea had the presence of mind to stick a couple of carrots in her pocket. She gave me one. I walked up to Babe and held it out. Babe seemed glad to see me and my carrot and stood, quietly, while I attached the lead rope to her halter. I was feeling like a real cowgirl. I had captured my mount. It took Lea only a few minutes to capture hers.

The farmer was not happy with us. Our horses had come through one of his cornfields, and he had reason to be upset. He wanted us gone and kept glaring.

Lea said, "Quick! Put on the bridle and let's get out of here! We'll ride the horses home and I'll bring you back in my car for the van."

My eyebrows shot up and I protested, "I've never ridden bareback. I don't know how! I can't get on without a stirrup!"

Lea sighed disgustedly. "Well, you're about to learn! Get your fat butt up onto that horse! You sit and steer! That's how you ride bareback!"

I put Babe's bridle over her halter and stood apprehensively. Lea cupped her hands and, when I put a foot into them, levered me up and onto Babe. Lea wasn't a very big woman, but I sailed up onto that horse in a heartbeat.

My heart was in my throat. Not only had I never ridden bareback, but we were riding on the road and that isn't the smartest place to do it for the first time. It can be very dangerous if drivers honk or swerve around you. Some horses spook under those conditions, and people have been known to die that way. I was writing my will in my head, and wishing I had put it down on paper.

I did fine until Lea picked up the pace and moved into a trot. I wobbled dangerously, from side to side, praying that I didn't hit the pavement. We made it home. I was sore for days and days. Apparently, riding bareback uses muscles that riding in a saddle does not.

A week later, Lea called. She had a deal we couldn't pass up. She had seen an ad for two ponies—a Shetland and a Pony of the Americas. They were free. All you had to do was take them home. Lea wanted the Shetland for her kids. She excitedly told me the bigger pony would be perfect for Sheri and Jason. She would keep both ponies until our barn was ready. Then, Babe and her companion could come home to our place. After all, I did have two stalls being built in the barn. Her enthusiasm was contagious.

It seemed like a terrific idea. I gathered Sheri and Jason, picked up Lea and her two boys, and we drove ten miles to the farmer's place. We examined the ponies. The Shetland was darling and perfect for Lea's young sons. The bigger pony was a pinto and his name was Macho. That name should have given me an idea of his attitude towards mares and life in general, but it did not.

The farmer said Macho's only problem was that he had only one testicle. What is it with the testicle thing? I thought, No big deal. I'll have him neutered like I did Frosty. Dr. Vet had found Frosty's retained testicle and removed it along with the other one. He could easily do the same with the pony. You horse people get a grip and stop laughing. Who knew horses and dogs don't share the same treatment for such things.

We agreed to take the ponies and realized we had a problem. The farmer wanted them gone now. He wasn't willing to keep them for even a couple of days. We didn't know anyone with a horse trailer. Lea and I had a conference and came up with a unique solution. Sheri could walk Macho home. Sheri enthusiastically agreed. I mean, how hard could it be to walk ten miles? How can fairly intelligent adults have no concept of how far ten miles really is, how long it will take to walk, and the limitations of a thirteen-year-old?

Sheri knew the way home. It was a simple route. Straight down the highway, through the town of East Troy, turn right, turn left, walk to our house. No problem. She set off with confidence.

Now for the Shetland. We decided she would fit in the van for the ride home. Hmmm. What if the cute pony gets nervous and makes a horsy mess on the floor of Bruce's favorite vehicle? I know! I asked the farmer for newspapers and covered the floor of the van. I figured, that's the way you protect the floor from dog accidents, the same should apply to possible horse accidents.

Lea and I levered the pony up and into the van. She took the heave-ho in stride and just fit behind the seat. I admit it was a bit tricky getting her front feet up high enough to access the van. But, a lift and shove did the trick. The pony seemed happy. She faced front and the kids petted her as she leaned across the back of the seat.

I drove toward home, then realized my gas tank was low. I pulled into the filling station. In those days, the attendants automatically wiped all the windows while they filled the tank. I watched the guy go around the van, washing windows. When he got to the back, he stopped, frowned, then continued to my window.

He lowered his voice and whispered, "Do you know you have a horse in your van?"

Like...how could I not know?

I nodded. He shook his head and said, "I have never seen a horse in a van before."

I was thinking, I doubt anyone has. As long as I can get the horse out before Bruce sees any of this, everything will be just fine. He's working until 8:00 tonight, so no problem.

We drove to Lea's, unloaded the pony by lifting her out, then waited for Sheri. Two hours later, no Sheri. It was starting to get dark and I was getting worried. By this time, Lea's husband, Sam, was home. We decided to drive the route and find Sheri.

We found Sheri and Macho as they were entering East Troy. Sheri was exhausted. It was obvious she was not going to make it home by dark. We parked the van alongside the road and had a conference. It was also obvious that even one of the adults could not walk Macho home before it got really dark. It was much too dangerous to be walking along country roads with a pony in the dark. We had to do something. Quick.

We decided to load Macho into the van. While loading the Shetland had been fairly easy, loading Macho was another matter. First of all, he was too tall for the van. We assessed that problem and decided, if he just bent his head down a little, he'd be okay. So Sheri got in the van and pulled the lead rope down to keep Macho from whacking his head on the van roof.

We put his front feet onto the back of the van. Macho said...no way! He quickly backed up. We tried again. When he bolted this time, he stepped backward. Lea's husband was trying to lift the pony's front feet into the van. Lea was cursing at the top of her lungs.

Her husband turned and reprimanded, "Lea! There are kids watching." (We had drawn a fairly sizeable crowd by this time.) "Watch your language and mouth!"

Lea sneered, "He's standing on my foot! Move him! Move him! If he were standing on your foot, you'd be cussing too! Owww!"

At that point, Lea and I got a good grip on Macho's hindquarters and levered him up and into the van. He was not happy. He started spinning around and the van rocked from side to side. Sam ordered us to close the van doors, and he got inside with Macho. Sam shouted for me to drive while he tried to calm down poor Macho.

The remaining drive was done at about ten miles an hour with the van rocking, Sam muttering, and Macho trying to escape. We decided to stop at my house, because it was closer, and keep Macho in the pasture overnight. He could be walked the short distance to Lea's in the morning. I pulled onto our driveway, and we quickly unloaded the pony, then led him to the pasture.

I glanced into the van and grimaced. The papers were strewn every which way and Macho had made a large deposit on the bench seat. Apparently, he had been facing toward the back of the van when nature called.

I left the back and sliding doors of the van open to air it out, thinking, I'll be right back to clean up that seat.

Sam, Lea, and I were standing admiring Macho and thanking God for getting us home safely as the sun set. I glanced toward the west, admired the streaks of pink and blue, and shuddered. Bruce had just pulled onto the driveway.

Uh-oh.

I thought, He'll just come over here. He'll never notice Macho's gift. Bruce never notices anything. Everything will be fine.

I watched my husband, dressed in his spiffy suit and carrying his briefcase, see us and wave. He started past the van, got to the side, sniffed the air, stopped, glanced in, and walked over to us.

Bruce made eye contact with me and said, "Is that what I think it is on the seat of the van?"

I smiled and batted my eyes. "Uhh. What do you think it is?"

Bruce shook his head. "Can't be. But, it looks like horse poop."

I rolled my eyes innocently and chuckled, "You're right. How could that be?"

Bruce studied Macho. "Where did he come from?"

I blurted, "I'll explain later."

Bruce looked into my eyes and said, "You can explain

why we have another horse when you explain why there's horse poop on the van seat!"

I blurted, "Got to go!" And dashed toward the kennel for the pooper-scooper.

Lucky for me Bruce is not a violent man.

I walked Macho over to Lea's the next day. My first concern was the one testicle. I didn't know anything about this problem in horses, but in dogs it was considered something that needed attention. Dogs that retain testicles were considered candidates for testicular cancer. I applied my past experience to my new one and decided that Macho had to be neutered and the retained testicle removed. I discovered our dog and cat vet didn't do horses. Lea got the number of the local farm vet from a neighbor.

I remember the conversation with my first farm vet.

Kathy: "I have a pony with one testicle. I want him neutered and the retained testicle removed."

Vet: "Umm. Neutered? You don't neuter a horse. You geld him."

Kathy: "Is geld the same as neuter?"

Vet: "Yep. Means you remove the testicle."

Kathy: "Okay, we agree on what we want done. So remove them."

Vet: "I won't be removing 'them.' I don't dig for retained testicles on my horses. I just take off the one that's hanging."

Kathy: "Aren't you afraid of cancer from the retained one?"

Vet: "Nope."

Kathy: "Are you sure that's medically sound procedure?"

Vet: "Yep."

Kathy: "Well, I'm not. I want the retained one taken out. I can't risk cancer."

Vet: "Never done that."

Kathy: "Well, can you do it?"

Vet: "Suppose so. Depends."

Kathy: "Depends on what?"

Vet: "Depends on whether I can do it or not."

Kathy: "Will you try?"

Vet: "Sure."

Kathy: "Do I bring him to your clinic?"

Vet: "I don't have a clinic. I make farm calls. I'll just come over and geld him."

Kathy: "Do I have to prepare a special place?"

Vet: "The front yard will do fine. Just tell me where."

I gave him Lea's address and asked what time he would be there.

Vet: "Don't know. Depends on what's going on. I'll be there sometime on Friday."

So much for scheduling. So much for pristine operating rooms.

I hung up, then made a few more calls to make sure the vet wasn't some kind of butcher or something. It turned out he was one of the most respected farm vets in the county. I wasn't convinced his methods were proper, but the people I talked to assured me that he knew what he was doing. I said a silent prayer for Macho and called Lea.

In the meantime, I was having a problem with my gang of Siberians. They had decided to howl each and every morning around 9:00. I would hear one lone mournful voice, then a chorus would join in. The routine was always the same. I would race to the bedroom window, throw it open, and glare out. The dogs I could see, except Kojak, would have their heads thrown back, voicing long, mournful howls. I would yell, "Hey, you guys! Knock it off!"

They would stop. Then, being the excellent dog trainer that I was, I would compliment the dog that was being good and not howling. "Good boy, Kojak!"

This went on for days. I could not understand why, all of a sudden, my gang was howling. Then, one day, I discovered the reason. I happened to glance out a few minutes before the usual howling session. Kojak meandered around his kennel, hopped up onto his bench, threw back his head, and howled. (The lone voice.) The other's would join in. (The chorus.) Then, Kojak looked expectantly toward the house.

I decided to do what I always did and bellowed, "Hey, you guys! Knock it off!"

The gang shut up. I waited a few seconds and watched Kojak. His tail started to wag. Then I said, "Good boy, Kojak!"

Do you see what was happening? Kojak had me trained to compliment him. Not only did he have me trained, he had the rest of his pack trained to get my attention. I had been outwitted for the umpteenth time by a critter!

Okay, time to get the upper hand. The next day, around the usual howling time, I confiscated the garbage can lid, sneaked around the corner of the house, hid, and waited. When Kojak tried to strike up the band with his lone vocalization, I hurled the lid at the fence. It clattered next to Kojak who, literally, jumped a foot. I snarled, "Kojak, No! Blast your little black heart! Knock it off!"

That was the end of the daily concert. I had won this round, but wondered how many I was losing without even knowing it.

On Friday morning, I decided to sleep later than usual. I was dozing when the phone rang. I frowned and glanced at the clock. It was only 7:30.

I answered. It was Lea. She quipped, "I've got your family jewels here in a bag."

"Huh?"

"Get your butt over here. The vet gelded Macho. I need help!"

I yawned. "But, it's only 7:30."

She sounded a tad sarcastic. "Oh, really? I didn't know that, probably because I've been helping the vet! Your pony is laying on my front yard for all the world to see. We gelded Macho with traffic driving past. The pony's unconscious and the vet said we've got to keep him quiet. Get over here!"

She hung up. I hurriedly dressed and drove over. Sure enough, Macho was sprawled at the entrance to her driveway. He looked dead to me. She had a blanket over his head. Lea explained that the vet instructed us to keep the pony quiet for as long as possible. Now, see, this is where interpretation of instructions can foul things up. What does...as long as possible...really mean?

The vet said when Macho began coming to, we were to hold him down until he calmed down and went back to sleep. The blanket covering his head would help with the calming part. If he couldn't see, he would just lay still. That was to make sure the wound had time to clot.

I didn't appreciate Lea displaying the "family jewels" to me in the bag. Apparently, the vet was amused by my insistence of wanting both, but was proud he managed to fill the order and wanted me to see that he had.

So, Lea and I stood there staring at the unconscious pony. We waited for a while, then decided coffee and doughnuts would help us take care of our patient. We gathered our goodies from her kitchen. Then, she got two buckets. We turned them over and used them for stools, then sat nibbling doughnuts and drinking steaming coffee.

We waited for an hour. Nothing happened. I thought maybe Macho had died. We took the blanket off and studied his face. I put my fingers in front of his nose and could feel air moving. Okay, he wasn't dead. We waited.

Another hour went by and Macho started twitching, then rolling from side to side. I asked, "How are we supposed to keep him down?"

Lea shook her head. "He didn't tell me how to do it."

We discussed what to do, then decided to just hold him down. She took the front end. I took the back. Macho thrashed around for a while, then gave it up.

Another hour passed and Macho woke up again. This time his thrashing was strong. Lea and I threw ourselves on him and held on for dear life.

I asked her how long we had to do this. She wasn't sure.

During the day, every time Macho showed signs of life, we would hurl ourselves onto his body and hang on until he dozed off. As time went on, Macho, of course, got stronger and stronger. He seemed to be unhappy with his state of affairs. But, then, so were we.

About 6:00 p.m., Sam pulled onto the driveway. At that time, Lea and I were laying across the pony's carcass.

He walked over to us and looked disgusted. "What in blazes are you two doing to that pony! Do you have any idea what that looks like from the road!"

Hmmm. We hadn't given what it looked like a thought. Maybe, because we were too busy hanging on for dear life!

Lea snarled something that I won't repeat because there might be young people reading this. Then, we babbled our explanation.

Sam looked thoroughly annoyed. "Well, I'm sure he didn't mean keep Macho down for the rest of his life! Did you ever think to call the vet and ask?"

Ummm. Nope. Too busy eating doughnuts, drinking coffee, and discussing husbands and their faults!

Sam marched into the house, made the call, then stomped back and lectured, "He meant for a few hours! Let that poor pony up!"

We took off the blanket and Macho struggled to his feet. He wobbled around the yard for a few minutes, then his eyes cleared and we put him in a stall. I suppose the pony had nightmares for years about being held down by unseen specters, but that's life. At least we took his mind off his loss.

The following week, I decided to bring both Babe and Macho home. Our barn would be completed in two weeks.

The weather report was for clear and sunny weather and, even if it did rain, it was summer. It was time to relieve Lea of her charges.

I rode Babe home, then retrieved Macho. Apparently, no one told Macho that he could no longer enjoy females. When I put him in the pasture with Babe, he had one thing on his mind. Love. Babe did not appreciate his advances and aimed several kicks in his direction. I spent a couple hours worrying that Macho would be killed, but he was very crafty at dodging blows. It looked to me as though he had plenty of experience. I now knew why he was called "Macho."

Babe and Macho never really hit it off. A few years later, she nailed him broadside with a good kick. That resulted in some internal bleeding, which resulted in a vet call, which resulted in blood being extracted from the swelling, which resulted in me giving Macho a shot of antibiotic every day for five days. I quivered at the thought of giving a pony a shot, but was informed the vet didn't come every day to give a mere shot. He showed me how to administer the shot. Smack the neck, insert the syringe, draw back to make sure you haven't hit a vein, and pump it in.

First day. Easy. Macho didn't see it coming.

Second day. Hold on tight! He's trying to get away!

Third day. Blast! Catch him, shove him against the side of the stall, and insert needle.

Fourth day. Tie him to the stall, use body to shove him to the side, hold on to head with one hand. Insert needle.

Fifth day. Chase him around stall, tie to post, shove, hold on, insert needle...ooops! Blood in the syringe! "Hold still! No! Oh, no! Look what all your antics made me do! I accidentally pumped the stuff into a vein! You'll drop dead!" Call the vet!

Kathy. Panting: "I pumped the medicine into his vein!"

Vet: "Is he walking around?"

Kathy: "Don't know!"

Vet: "Go look."

I ran to the barn, checked the pony, and ran back.

Kathy. Gasping: "He's walking around!"

Vet: "Then, he's okay. If he wasn't, he'd be belly up in the dirt, feet in the air. You got nothing to worry about."

I suppose there was logic to that.

As our barn neared completion, I realized I needed some kind of fill for the stalls. Keeping the horses on dirt flooring didn't seem like a good idea. I needed a base that would drain and decided on sand. I called the sand company and told the guy how much area I needed to fill. He suggested six yards should fill two 12´x12´ stalls just fine. Seeing as how my math skills have always been sub-standard, I took his word for it. It seemed that three yards in each stall should do the trick.

The next day, the sand truck backed up to our corral and dumped its load.

"Stop! Wait! You can't leave all that sand! My God! There's tons of it! I only need six yards."

As I babbled to the truck driver, pleading that there had been a mistake, he politely told me it was six cubic yards, not six yards. It's not possible to measure a flat six yards of dirt, sand, gravel, or anything else. You do cubic yards. Any idea of how much sand is in six cubic yards? Lots.

Bruce almost came unhinged when he saw the huge pile. To his credit, he had been handling everything pretty well up to then. He sneered that it would take years to fill the stalls and he had other plans for the weekend! He'd get to it when he got to it!

Well, that seems a bit testy. Would you like a drink?

The next day, I stood, staring at the pile, and decided I could fill those stalls myself. I knew how to shovel snow. Sand couldn't be all that much different. I could fill the wheelbarrow, push it into the barn, dump the sand into a stall, then rake it smooth. How hard could that be? It certainly wouldn't take a rocket scientist. What I did discover, though, was it took a strong back and arms. Stubbornly I worked on that pile without telling Bruce. It took days and days and days.

Because the sandpile and the stall doors were behind the garage and on the edge of the lot facing the neighbors, Bruce couldn't see it during every day activities. So, I didn't get busted.

I shoveled sand and shoveled sand and shoveled sand. I got so I hated that stuff. I still hate that stuff. After adding about ten inches of sand to each stall, I still had a huge pile. So, I decided to even it off and fill the corral with sand. Good plan!

Now, I raked and raked and raked.

On Saturday, I smugly took Bruce to the barn and showed him my accomplishment. He was annoyed because, with my back problems, I shouldn't have been shoveling, wheelbarrowing, or raking. Then, he was annoyed with my impatience.

Who's impatient?

Then, he grumbled he was going to do it if I would just have waited!

Where was the compliment!

Slow in coming, but eventually it did. However, it was not long in duration or sincerity.

A few days later, Sheri came running in, screaming. Frosty was chasing Babe and Macho around the pasture. Yikes! Macho kicks!

I dashed out and charged toward the pasture. Sure enough, our milk truck hitchhiker had finally found some critters to chase. And, they were big ones.

Babe and Macho were galloping just out of the yapping Frosty's reach. All I could think about was the kind of blows those horses were capable of delivering. Suddenly,

Macho turned and charged at Frosty. The Westie, completely undaunted, sidestepped and went after Babe. She seemed to think his antics were mildly amusing and toyed with him, staying just out of reach.

I called, "Frosty, come!" until I turned blue. I suppose I shouldn't have been surprised that the idiot didn't come. After all, he was on a mission!

I crawled through the pasture fence and joined the chase. Babe was galloping just ahead of Macho who was tossing his head and snorting. Frosty was yapping, little legs churning, just behind Macho. I was panting and calling right behind Frosty.

The horses broke rank and took off in separate directions. Frosty, little pink tongue hanging down to his toes, was slowing down. He was, however, still yapping. I got to him just before Macho did. I whisked Frosty into my arms and headed for the fence. In spite of the fact that Frosty could hardly catch his breath, he kept yapping away. He was saying, "Next time I'm going to get you!"

For several weeks, the daring Frosty was kept tied when put outside. When let loose, he would head straight for the pasture and his varmints.

We had several trainer-trainee discussions over his behavior and, in the end, Frosty decided to stay out of the pasture!

A few days later, we had a minor crisis in what had become a daily crisis of some sort or other. Our neighbor called and said he thought Babe was stuck in the wire fence separating our properties.

In addition to Babe not liking Macho, she truly hated the neighbor's mare who enjoyed hanging out under a tree against the fence. The fencing between our properties was typical woven wire pasture fence stapled to wooden posts.

We rushed outside and, sure enough, Babe was caught in the fence. She had turned her backside to the neighbor's mare and tried to land a double kick broadside. Instead of making contact with her unfavorite neighbor, Babe's back legs had gone through the fence. She was literally wired into the fence.

Babe stood very quietly as we inspected her dilemma. We had no clue as to what to do. Many horses, in this type situation, panic and can do terrible damage to themselves and anyone standing close. But, Babe was calm as though trusting us to help her.

Bruce finally decided to get a wire cutter and try to cut her out. That meant cutting wire around the mare's back legs all the way up to her belly. Any horse person will tell you that was a very dangerous tactic, but we were novices and didn't understand what could have happened.

The wire was thick and didn't cut easily. Bruce had to put the wire cutter against Babe's skin, wiggle it under, then snip the wire and hope the wire didn't cut her. He also had to bend down right in front of those powerful legs.

I held Babe's head and gently stroked her, telling her we were only trying to help and I hope she understood. I grimaced each time I heard a wire snap and worried about Bruce.

Babe never flinched. When she was finally free, she rubbed her nose against my chest and walked forward. She never thanked Bruce, who had the task of rewiring the fence back together. Incidentally, the "rewiring" thing is arduous and the fence is never the same. It looks like a puzzle that has been put together wrong. Ultimately, we had to take out one whole section of wire and replace it.

Babe and Bruce had issues. He liked her. He rode her. She liked him too. He provided her with amusement. Her favorite game was to work to dislodge him by charging under trees and trying to wipe him off her back. She never used that tactic with me, but loved trying to unseat Bruce. Babe would calmly let him climb into the saddle, begin a trot around the pasture, get up to full speed and head for the trees lining the perimeter. Bruce would frantically rein her to the side, and she'd gleefully keep going as branches smacked his head and shoulders. Who says horses do not have a sense of humor? She did not, however, seem to have a sense of gratitude.

I watched Babe frolic in the pasture and realized she was, once again, trying to pick a fight with the neighbor's mare. I was worried Babe would repeat her kicking and end up stuck again. I talked over my dilemma with Lea and she suggested using hot wire as a deterrent. That seemed like a good idea to me.

We went to our favorite hardware store and bought one battery, a grounding stake, hundreds of feet of wire, and conduits for each post. For those of you who are unfamiliar with "hot wire," it's a method used to give a slight shock to any livestock that touches it. The installation was fairly simple. You mount the battery to one post. You pound in a conduit to each wood fence post. The conduits were ceramic spools. Then, you loop the wire around each conduit. You hook the wire to the battery, string wire around the pasture's perimeter, and end up back where you started.

Of course, there were a zillion wooden fence posts, so Lea and I spent several afternoons pounding in conduits, then stringing the wire. When we were finished, we stood proudly in the pasture, admiring our work. We had lined the entire inside of the pasture fence. I thought, smugly, That should keep Babe away from the fence.

We ambled over to the battery. Lea was babbling about something. I was ignoring her as I savored the moment of turning on my awesome new fence. I leaned over, flipped the switch, and Lea shouted, "No! Don't hold onto the grounding stake at the same time!"

Too late. I was shocked by my own "hot wire" and was now sitting on my fanny. I could attest to the fact that the fence was "hot." I have no idea what possessed me to grab onto that stake. It might have been for balance as I wobbled off the rock that I stumbled over. Who knows? That incident probably put my guardian angel back in psychoanalysis.

Only my pride was injured. The shock was strong enough to zap me onto my behind, but didn't leave any lasting damage. But, I was convinced the pulsing wire would keep Babe at bay. After all, it was sure going to keep me at bay.

The next morning, I looked out, enjoying the view, and frowned. Babe was standing next to her unfavorite mare. The hot wire had been pulled down for about one hundred feet to allow her access. I could not believe my eyes.

I spent a couple hours reattaching it. And, yes, I did have sense enough to turn off the power. I was also careful when I turned it back on.

The next day the wire was down again. This went on for several days. Then, I gave up and removed all the wire, deciding if that blasted horse wanted to get herself wired up again, she should go for it! Now, you can add "horse" to the list of critters who have outsmarted me.

It was a beautiful Saturday morning. Bruce was doing a few yard chores. The construction guys were putting the finishing touches on our barn. I was bored as I watched Macho and Babe graze in the pasture. In my mind, I envisioned riding down some trail enjoying Babe, the sun, and wind. Then, it hit me. I could go for a horseback ride. But, where? I know. We'll ride over to Mae and Pete's. I'll surprise them by trotting up their driveway, having a cold soda, and riding back home. What a great way to spend a day.

I should call Mae and tell her I'm coming. No! A surprise will be more fun.

I told Bruce I was taking Babe and going for a visit. He warned me it was fifteen miles to Mae's and said, "Isn't that a long way to ride a horse?"

I answered, "No. It's only a twenty minute drive, so it

can't take all that long to ride over."

Why did I not have any concept about time, miles, speed, etc? Is it a spatial issue? Or, a severe lack of logic? Or, just plain ignorance? Or, was it always overconfidence?

Any thinking person can figure out that when you drive at sixty miles per hour and ride at about four miles per hour, there will be a difference in time on the road. I never did get that old algebra problem about the trains, speeds, and so on. Perhaps I should have practiced until I understood what it all meant. I guess I wasn't thinking that day. It seemed "not thinking" was an ongoing problem.

When Sheri found out I was going for a ride, she begged to come with me. She was an experienced horsewoman and often rode Macho.

The thought of a mother/daughter adventure was exciting. So, we saddled up and headed down the driveway. Bruce and the construction guys were laughing. They said we wouldn't make it. They said we'd be back within the hour. They said no way were we going to make it to Mae's.

Remember the "team training?" Remember the challenge? Well, another gauntlet had been thrown down. I decided I would show them all.

Sheri and I enjoyed the first hour. The second hour was proving painful. The third hour, neither one of us could stand being in the saddle anymore. Also, Macho was limping. Neither Babe nor Macho wore horseshoes and being on the pavement was making them footsore. Even though we were moving from the tarred road to the dirt shoulder, the ride was taking its toll. Sheri and I got off and led the horses onward.

There is no way I would have turned back. My mother used to say, "Pride goeth before the fall." She was right.

We finally limped up Mae's driveway. She was surprised to see us, all right. In fact, Mae and Pete were in the middle of a project and unannounced guests weren't on their agenda. I regretted not calling in advance. But, we were invited for our sodas, and as I sat sipping it, conversing with my friends, all I could think about was the ride home. Every muscle in my body ached, Sheri was tired, and both horses were limping.

Mae and Pete did not have horse facilities, so leaving the horses overnight was not an option. I hated the idea of calling Bruce and admitting I had made a mistake.

Pete assessed the horses and asked if I really thought I could ride them home. I shrugged and said I'd have to walk them home. Riding wasn't an option. The horses weren't up for it and neither were Sheri and I.

Pete hit on an idea. He knew the farmer down the road and thought the guy had a horse trailer. So, we hopped into Pete's car and drove over.

The German Shepherd wouldn't let us out of the car. He threw himself against the doors and barked. The farmer ambled out and called the dog off. Pete told me not to get out of the car, he would talk to the guy.

No problem. I wasn't up to being eaten by a rogue dog. I hurt enough already.

Pete worked out an agreement with the farmer and they hooked the trailer to his car. We drove back to pick up the horses.

We loaded Macho without a problem. He didn't mind the trailer. Apparently, it was quite an improvement over his ride in the van.

But...we had a problem with Babe. It seems the farmer raised ponies and my horse didn't quite fit. Her rump was a bit too plump. Pete and I talked the problem over and realized it was getting late in the afternoon, and we didn't have any options. We made an executive decision and crunched Babe into the trailer, then slammed the tailgate.

I could see we weren't going to have to worry about her shifting her weight. She was a tight fit, but she was a fit.

Pete drove us home. I can still see the look on Bruce and the construction guys faces when we pulled onto our driveway with the trailer in tow. Their laughter still rings in my ears. They were chortling about the horses needing a ride and how that was a new way to go for a trail "ride!"

As I unloaded the horses, I snapped, "Hah! We did make it to Mae's and back. And, a ride's a ride!"

I have never forgotten Pete's kindness that day. He never lectured me for being foolish, although I'm sure he was thinking that very thing and biting back the words. He went out of his way to help a friend who used poor judgment. For that, I'll always be grateful.

We had many, many more adventures during our time in the country. Eventually, we moved to a bigger property, with a huge kennel and barn. We bred Siberians, added a Samoyed, Doberman, Alaskan Malamutes, and another horse and pony to our group. Every day was a challenge. Every day there was a minor crisis of some sort. Some of the crises were not minor. I've been often asked, why did we do it? Why would we want to spend so much time working so hard?

How do you explain passion for a lifestyle? How do explain that the work doesn't matter when you're doing something you love?

Let me try.

I absolutely loved every dog, horse, cat, or critter we ever owned. Each was an individual spirit with a lesson to teach. They brought so much joy into our lives, it was worth every moment of work. I learned to share myself with these animals. I taught them and they taught me. I truly enjoyed the challenge of training and providing adequate care. I learned about responsibility. I was given companionship and unconditional love even when I fouled up. Did I make mistakes? Yes. But, a wise person once told me that there are no mistakes. Only experiences from which to learn. I tried to learn. And, I am still learning to this day.

I came to realize that, when I began, I was uneducated about many things. That I should have put more time and effort into learning what was required to take care of these animals, with whom we share the Earth, before taking on the responsibility.

Most of us get caught up in the idea of having a pet. And, true, it is wonderful to have a companion or companions. But, we must understand what kind of commitment is required. We need to know about nutrition, health care, grooming, training, and the amount of companionship that our pets need. They are like innocent children who look to us to fill their needs. If we don't understand what those needs are...we will fail these loving, trusting creatures. The shelters are filled with animals that have been "failed."

If we're not willing to put in the time to learn and teach, then we must reconsider the decision to add a pet to our family. Animals do not walk into our homes ready to do our bidding. We don't expect our children to take on life without teaching them. Think of the time and effort it takes to bring a child into society. Why would bringing an animal into an "alien" society require any less?

And, to breed them requires even more commitment. I always felt that any puppy bred by me was always welcome back. Think about what that means. That means if you produce them, you are responsible for them their entire life. That means they will never end up in a shelter. Dedicated breeders often are very active in dog rescue groups. And, that means rescuing dogs they did not produce, many of whom were produced irresponsibly.

And, where would breeders be without the caring, loving pet person? The person who loves a breed and wants to share their home with them? Dogs I bred found wonderful homes. People sent me letters and photos, and I loved getting them.

This book is about the silly things I did as I enjoyed my animals. It's about the way I learned. Always the hard way. Hopefully, I did not learn at the expense of my animals—only at my own expense. As I look back, I regret not taking time to look and learn before I leapt. If you're reading this book and thinking about a pet, my heartfelt advice is: read, learn, talk to those who know and, most importantly, listen. It's easy to fall in love with a unique blue-eyed Siberian Husky, a lovely German Shepherd, a cute Maltese, or a pretty Poodle. But, those physical traits often mask temperaments that are not compatible with your own.

Siberians are loyal, loving, smart, and teachable. They love to run. Terriers are bred to chase. German Shepherds are extremely intelligent. Australian Shepherds live to herd. Poodles and the Maltese need hours of grooming. My question to you is: Do you want to spend time running? Chasing a Terrier? Grooming and brushing tangled hair? Are you capable of outthinking a German Shepherd? Do you understand the gentle nip of a herding dog is intended to "herd" you and not hurt you? Buy with your intelligence, not with your ego, and your new friend will fit perfectly into your family.

There were times I had to euthanize dogs I bred and loved. Sometimes, circumstances arise that make this decision necessary. I agonized over every dog I ever put down. There are those who think it is never appropriate to take this drastic step. I would disagree. There is a time it is appropriate. And that is to alleviate pain. There are many kinds of pain—physical, emotional, spiritual. To allow an animal to suffer, in order to spare myself the agony of making a final decision, was not acceptable to me. I grieved over every one I euthanized, and I take full responsibility for every decision I made. Before that decision was made, I talked with vets, analyzed the animal's behavior, then assessed the pain level and quality of life. I never...never...put down a dog for convenience's sake. I decided, in the beginning, that if euthanizing ever became easy, it was time to get out of dogs, forever.

Many people laugh at those in the sport of dogs. They watch Westminster and it seems silly the way the dogs are primped, pampered, and pranced around a ring. You don't see what takes place behind the scenes. Dedicated breeders are sitting in the stands, watching. They're comparing their breeding with that of others. They're trying to decide how to improve their breeds. They're comparing their dogs to the standard. They discuss, analyze, argue, criticize, and make important decisions. Are there those just in it for the money and prestige of winning? Of course. But, the majority are dedicated dog lovers intent on making a difference.

And, I submit to you, that the dog show world is where I learned so many things. I learned about myself—my flaws and my strengths. I learned about politics. I learned that people who say the most, sometimes know the least. Often, those who sit and ponder are the ones you should ask questions. I learned to observe, then trust my judgment and not rely on the words of someone else. I learned that dedicated breeders will always help a novice. Always. There are no dumb questions.

I learned about sharing a passion. I met caring people. Also, I met people who put emphasis on winning and forgot the joy of competing. Did that happen to me? For a while—yes. That's not something I'm proud to admit. It's easy to get caught up in winning. However, I discovered that I learned much more from losing. I saw child competitors berate their animals when they lost and admonished my children to never emulate that behavior. I saw the same thing in adults and the lesson was—why do we often blame others for our failures?

We traveled and met people we never would have encountered in a normal life. We shared joy and sadness with strangers who empathized.

Our children learned about the responsibility of pet ownership. Our family motto was: If you have a pet, his needs come first, yours come second.

Our family shared the responsibility of caring for our critters. We shared the joy of birth and the grief of death.

Sheri and Jason worked hard in the kennel, keeping things clean, feeding dogs and horses, loading and unloading tons of dog food and hay. The four of us shared our love of each other, love of the animals, and joy of what we accomplished. We all contributed to our lifestyle and made it possible. I wanted our children to understand that their contributions were every bit as important as their Dad's and mine.

The four of us share a bond to this day. A bond forged on a few acres, chasing dogs and horses, in the country long ago. I am extremely proud of Sheri, Jason, and Bruce. We all matured in that place. We loved, learned, and shared. What more can a mother, or wife, ask?

I remember Bruce holding a newborn puppy in his hands, lovingly cradling it. I remember the smell of a newborn pup as I let it sniff my chin. I saw new canine mothers shelter their puppies much like a human mother would. I watched a pack of dogs interact and learn from each other. I experienced the love and trust of my animal charges. We shared life and death. We shared winning and losing. We shared success and failure. We shared the beauty of nature as the sled skimmed over a crust of snow in a silent forest crowned with a blanket of white.

What is the greatest gift I received from a kennel full of dogs, a hunting cat, and a pasture of horses?

Unconditional love.

For that—I'll always be grateful.

Dedication

This book is lovingly dedicated to my animal friends:

My beloved Siberian Huskies:
Apricot Brandie
American, Canadian Champion Boettcher's Natasha
American, Canadian Champion Amorak's Baku of Bruka
American, Canadian Champion Bruka's Kojak of Catca
American, Canadian Champion Bruka's Tanta of Catca
Bruka's Apuka of Catca
Bruka's Tabu of Catca
American, Canadian Champion Bruka's Sentinal Haznosput
American, Canadian Champion Bruka's Phantom Howler, CD
American Champion Headwind's Renegade of Bruka
Canadian Champion Bruka's Lone Wolf
Canadian Champion Bruka's Spring Flower

Our loyal West Highland White Terriers:
Boettcher's Jack Frost, CD
Marantha's Miss Bewitchin (Pixie)

Our joyous Alaskan Malamutes:
Shara
American Champion Win-Kre's Akamai Fury, WD
Dejah

Our dedicated guardian Doberman Pinscher:
Raven

Our fierce hunter:
Tiger the cat

Our equine companions:
Babe
Macho

The dog who brought us out of the depths of sorrow—Buford Butz. The most incredible Norwich Terrier you will ever meet.

And, to our newest addition:
Angel. A Maltese who has the heart of a lion, the intelligence of many humans, and the loving spirit of an angel.

A Special Thank You

An author usually thanks everyone at the beginning of a story. But, by now, you certainly are aware that I often do not do things the "usual" way. There is a reason I chose to make these thank-yous in this place. I wanted you to meet and personally know the people I am about to thank.

Bruce Boettcher has encouraged and enjoyed my eccentric personality from the time we were teenagers. We recently celebrated our forty-year anniversary. He makes me laugh when I am moaning about not being "normal" and want to stop writing. Bruce made this book possible by pressing me to tell about my experiences after helping me create them with his own bare hands, love, and patience. He was enduring chemotherapy during the writing of this book, but managed to edit it and encourage me. He is the true definition of "courage," and I love him with all my heart.

Sheri Boettcher suggested I write this book. When I argued, she insisted. I did not want to write it because I was certain no one would enjoy a look into my own personal past. She vehemently disagreed and had the courage to tell me so. That's not as simple as it sounds. I have a rather strong personality. Sheri has been a joy in my life from the moment she opened her blue eyes and looked into mine. I treasure her sense of humor and wonderful laugh. We share a love of animals, but she has dog "sense" that I do not possess. She is a sensitive, loving woman who I love with all my heart.

Jason Boettcher is my chief critic. After I soothe my tattered ego, I always end up taking his excellent suggestions. His wonderful sense of humor is a joy to experience, and he's been making me smile from the time he first tried to outwit me with a grin and a joke. When I was baffled by an uncooperative computer, he saved wear and tear on my frazzled nerves with his computer expertise. When Jason has a dog in his lap, his eyes are filled with love, and I have pictures of him as a child holding a puppy with the same look on his face. He's a loving, compassionate man, and I love him with all my heart.

Ruby Marshall and Jason were married a few months ago. She is an outspoken young woman who I adore. When she told me the book was a "fun read," she made my day. Welcome to our family, Ruby.

Thank you all for joining me in this life and accepting me for what and who I am.

Kathy and Mom

Last Words

It is my fervent hope that you enjoyed my experiences and through our sharing, come to realize the importance of educating yourself when considering acquiring a pet of any kind. Pet ownership is a responsibility that gives us many rewards. But, it also requires dedication.

If you're thinking about a new animal family member, and are not interested in showing a purebred, check with local Humane Societies and Animal Shelters. They have wonderful animals looking for homes.

Purebred breeders can be found through local kennel clubs and breed clubs. I suggest you check breeders' references before purchasing an animal.

There are numerous Purebred Dog Rescue Groups looking for homes for their special breeds. The American Kennel Club website has a listing of Purebred Dog Breed Clubs. Those breed clubs, as well as local kennel clubs, can put you in contact with rescue groups. The dogs that come through those rescue groups are thoroughly evaluated for health and temperament. Both Buford and Angel came from rescue situations.

And lastly, please neuter and spay your animals. Anyone interested in showing does not have that option, but that is a very small percentage of dog owners. Please do not breed unless you fully understand the impact your act will have, not only upon your breed, but upon the entire pet population. Remember...you are responsible for the lives you create.

May your experiences with animals bring you the same love and joy that has filled my heart. Remember this always...**the way we treat our animals reveals our inner spirit.**

Kathy Boettcher

About the Author

Kathy's journey into the world of dogs began, simply enough, with the purchase of a family puppy. That challenging acquisition led her into dog training, grooming, and eventually, into the realm of dog showing. Born and raised in Waukesha, Wisconsin, she was a content city girl until dogs entered her life. A growing pack of dogs necessitated a move into farm country—a lifestyle change that had great appeal for Kathy, but she had no practical experience in country living. Learning "the ropes" proved challenging.

In the span of a decade, Kathy went from owning one obstinate West Highland White Terrier to a kennel full of canine companions. She enrolled in obedience classes, learned to groom, and took conformation classes. The family raised two Westies, a Samoyed, a Doberman Pinscher, several Alaskan Malamutes, and cats. She bred, raised, trained, and showed Siberian Huskies. A horse and pony completed the family circle.

Competing in obedience and conformation, Kathy and her daughter, Sheri, ultimately finished six American Canadian champions, two American champions, several Canadian champions, two obedience champions, and two Best In Show Siberian Husky Teams.

Kathy judged conformation and Junior Showmanship at fun matches, taught conformation classes, and was a member of the Siberian Husky Club of Greater Milwaukee, the Waukesha Kennel Club, and the Siberian Husky Club of America.

Kathy is now a novelist who lives in San Diego, California. Her current canine companions are a Norwich Terrier named Buford Butz and a Maltese named Angel.

If you would like additional copies of Our Doggie Delinquents, please fill out the order form listed below and mail to:

CELEEN PUBLISHING
Dog Tales Division
P. O. Box 928049
San Diego, CA 92192-8049

You may also contact us via:

Phone: **858-547-0189**
E-mail: **sales@celeen.com**
www.celeen.com

Copies of Our Doggie Delinquents @ $15.95 = __________

Shipping and handling = __________
($4.00 for the first book, $2.00 each additional copy)

California residents 7¾% sales tax = __________

TOTAL = __________

The sequel to *Our Doggie Delinquents, Did We Reform Them? Or Did They Reform Us?* will be released in Spring, 2004. It is entitled *More Doggie Delinquents-Still Not Reformed* and continues the family's challenges and adventures with their animals and country living. If you would like to be notified when it is due for release, please contact Celeen Publishing, Dog Tales Division at the above address.

The third and final book in the Our Doggie Delinquents series is scheduled for release in late Summer 2004.

Kathleen Boettcher is also a novelist. Her science fiction, romance adventure entitled *Eesoo* can be purchased through Celeen Publishing or on Amazon.com. This is mature reading.

Six romance novels based upon *Eesoo* are due to be released in Winter 2004. If you are interested in being notified when these books are released, please contact Celeen Publishing at the above address.